AMERICAN
HERITAGE

April 1964 · Volume XV, Number 3

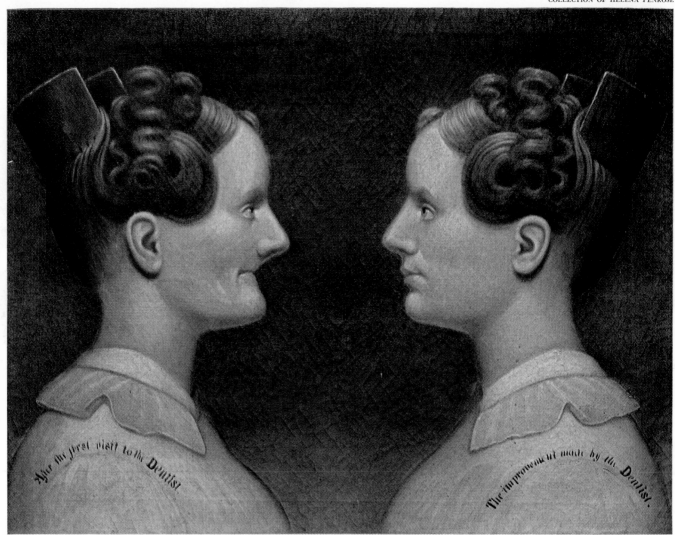

It is not clear whether the great increase in pulchritude, left to right above, is attributable to a superior set of false teeth, or to a pioneering orthodontic triumph. At any rate, the painting, which was among the effects of a nineteenth-century dentist in Chatham, Massachusetts, is one of the earlier examples of the before-and-after technique in advertising. Does she or doesn't she? Which twin has the tony dentures? The anonymous commercial artist made sure that everyone could tell.

AMERICAN HERITAGE

The Magazine of History

PUBLISHER
James Parton
EDITORIAL DIRECTOR
Joseph J. Thorndike, Jr.
SENIOR EDITOR
Bruce Catton

EDITOR
Oliver Jensen
MANAGING EDITOR
Robert L. Reynolds
ASSOCIATE EDITORS
Robert Cowley
E. M. Halliday
Richard M. Ketchum
Joan Paterson Mills
ASSISTANT EDITORS
Lyndall Dyer
Stephen W. Sears
CONTRIBUTING EDITOR
Barbara Klaw
LIBRARIAN
Caroline Backlund
COPY EDITOR
Beverly Hill
ASSISTANT: Suzanne Smith

SENIOR ART DIRECTOR
Irwin Glusker
ART DIRECTOR
Murray Belsky
STAFF PHOTOGRAPHER: Herbert Loebel

ADVISORY BOARD
Allan Nevins, *Chairman*

Carl Carmer   Louis C. Jones
Gerald Carson   Alvin M. Josephy, Jr.
Marshall B. Davidson   Harry Shaw Newman
John A. Garraty   Howard H. Peckham
Eric F. Goldman   Francis S. Ronalds
S. K. Stevens

AMERICAN HERITAGE is published every two months by American Heritage Publishing Co., Inc., 551 Fifth Avenue, New York, N.Y. 10017. Correspondence about subscriptions should be addressed to: American Heritage Subscription Office, 383 West Center Street, Marion, Ohio. Single Copies: $3.95. Annual Subscriptions: $15.00 in U.S. & Canada; $16.00 elsewhere.

An annual Index of AMERICAN HERITAGE is published every February, priced at $1.00. A Cumulative Index of Volumes VI–X is available at $3.00.

AMERICAN HERITAGE will consider but assumes no responsibility for unsolicited material.
Title registered U.S. Patent Office.
Second class postage paid at New York, N.Y., and at additional mailing offices.

Sponsored by

American Association for State & Local History · Society of American Historians

CONTENTS *April, 1964 · Volume XV, Number 3*

COVER: The artist—one A. A. Lamb, about whom almost nothing is known—painted this 1865 tribute to the Emancipation Proclamation with a suitably unfettered imagination. To the cheers of a throng of ex-slaves whose manacles have been broken, Abraham Lincoln presents the great document of 1863 from the back of a splendid charger—perhaps more gracefully than long-legged Abe might have done in reality. He is escorted by a choice segment of the Union Army, and heralded by a Goddess of Liberty who appears to have driven her chariot straight out of a Grecian frieze. (An article on one of the great setbacks to the process of full emancipation—the Supreme Court decision in *Plessy v. Ferguson*, 1896—begins on page 52.) Presented by Edgar William Garbisch and Bernice Chrysler Garbisch to the National Gallery of Art, the picture now hangs in the Treaty Room of the White House. *Back Cover:* As crowded as a Victorian parlor, this poster for Chicago's Columbian Exposition could still merely hint at the myriad marvels that awaited the visitor to the big world's fair of 1893—quite possibly more astonishing, in their time, than anything in store at New York in 1964. The poster is from a collection in the Library of Congress.

An exile from his own land, ex-Senator William Gwin dreamed of lost mines in Sonora,

an Eldorado for unreconstructed Confederates, and a title in Maximilian's Mexico

THE EMPERORS

By LATELY THOMAS

Early in 1863 there appeared in the cozy circle of Confederate agents and sympathizers in Paris a southern gentleman whose looks were fully as distinguished as his reputation. Erect and tall—he stood six feet two—with a massive head crowned by a backswept plume of iron-gray hair, he had aquiline features, a penetrating glance, and a hard, resolute mouth. He carried himself with an air of authority; though he was the son of a Tennessee frontier preacher, he had the bearing and manners of a born aristocrat.

This arrival from the seceded states was William McKendree Gwin, a man who had been in his remarkable and wide-ranging lifetime a lawyer, a doctor, a land speculator, a wealthy cotton planter, a congressman from Mississippi, a founder of the state of California, and one of its first two senators. Now he was about to embark on an enterprise more grandiose than any so far—for Gwin would not only grasp at a dukedom in Maximilian's Mexico and a fortune beyond reckoning, but he would attempt to provide a faltering Confederacy with a sanctuary in a new country.

The Doctor, as he was called, although he had abandoned medical practice years before, had reached the French capital after a long, circuitous, and often hazardous journey. When his Senate term had expired in March, 1861, Gwin had deemed it the better part of wisdom to retire to his San Francisco home, out of the public eye. In the frantic days before Sumter, he had acted as a go-between in a clandestine correspondence carried on by Jefferson Davis and Lincoln's Secretary of State, William Henry Seward; trying to play both sides, he had ended being trusted by neither. If his sympathies were with the South, he had little taste for

secession and open warfare. Gwin was too much a man of the world to become a rabid partisan.

Gwin had not remained in California long. In October, he had returned to the East for a reunion with his family. But his southern affiliations proved his undoing: during the lengthy sea journey by way of Panama, Union officers sailing with him had accused the ex-Senator of having treasonable communications with the enemy, and had arrested him. Upon his arrival in New York, Gwin was imprisoned for ten days, but the charges were too vague to stick, and after a hearing in Washington, he had been released.

Still professing to be neutral in the national struggle, the Doctor had headed south for the plantation he owned in Mississippi, and there he remained all through 1862; ostensibly he was occupied in cataloguing his extensive collection of congressional documents. Late that year, however, Grant had begun his thrust toward Vicksburg; the Gwin plantation lay directly in the path of the advancing Union army. Its owner did not tarry to welcome the Yankees. In the winter of 1863, he took passage aboard the block-

In the haughty, rough-hewn face of William McKendree Gwin (opposite) there was the look of one accustomed to command, persuade, and manipulate. Gwin's imagination was fired by tales of the vast quantities of precious metals the Spanish had taken from the Mexican earth. The depiction at right of a silver mine was done by the explorer Samuel de Champlain during a trip to Mexico in 1599–1601.

ade runner *Robert E. Lee,* which slipped out of the harbor of Wilmington, North Carolina, and outdistanced a pursuing Federal cruiser. Thus William McKendree Gwin arrived safely in Paris, to take up residence on the fashionable Boulevard Malesherbes.

He found life in the glittering, light-hearted capital of Napoleon III's Second Empire brisk and pleasant; the colony of Confederates which he joined was popular with society as well as with the government. Still, the Doctor had more serious concerns than attending soirées and dinner parties. At fifty-nine, he was a man without a country, in search of a new career. But he was also a master of political finesse, and the web of intrigue in which he soon became enmeshed was entirely to his liking. It was not long before he spotted an opportunity that promised adequate employment for his abundant gifts of leadership and organization.

Paris just then was agog over recent events in Mexico, where Napoleon III had embarked upon a grandiose scheme: stage-managing an empire. Ever since the overthrow of Spanish rule, Mexico had been racked by revolutions and wars. Its treasury was bankrupt, its foreign debts unpaid. Then, in 1861, Great Britain, France, and Spain lost patience and sent a joint expeditionary force to occupy Veracruz. But Napoleon had more far-reaching plans than a punitive seizure of one port, and when the British and Spaniards caught his drift, they hastily withdrew. The French army remained, and under the pretext of "pacifying" the land, routed the ragged troops of Mexico's President Benito Juárez. Napoleon's ambition was to create a sphere of French influence in Central America which would eventually extend from Texas to Peru; Mexico would be an immediate source of needed raw materials and a rich market for French manufactures. His choice for the throne of this new empire was the handsome, mild-mannered Hapsburg prince, Archduke Maximilian, brother of Emperor Franz Josef of Austria.

All this was of great interest to the Doctor. As a senator, Gwin had studied the history and topography of Mexico, and one evening at the home of a fellow expatriate he spoke at length of the supposedly vast and hardly touched mineral riches of the state of Sonora. In that mountainous, sparsely populated, and almost unexplored region lying to the south of the Arizona Territory, Gwin said, fabulous wealth could be found in a maze of forgotten or abandoned mines. A fascinated listener was the Marquis de Montholon, former French consul in New York and Napoleon's newly appointed minister to Mexico. Montholon was a member of the inner circle at the Tuileries, and like most educated Frenchmen spoke English fluently, that language being the current idiom of sport, dandyism, and high fashion. Gwin, relieved of the necessity of relying upon the scanty provincial French he had acquired in New Orleans, talked freely and eloquently.

In the eighteenth century, he told the Marquis, Sonora had been reconquered from the Spaniards by roving bands of warlike Indians—Yaquis, Apaches, and other tribes—who since that time had defied both Spanish and Mexican authority. In the colonial period the mines of Sonora, especially those yielding gold and silver, had ranked among the richest known; but when the Indians took over the country, the mines had been abandoned, the very location of some being lost to record. The almost incalculable wealth of the Sierra Madre might be estimated from colonial account books. For instance, there was the legendary Tayopa ("the mine with the iron door"), lost somewhere in the Sonora wastelands; it was believed to be the richest single deposit of precious metals in the world. In the same region lay the Minas Prietas, and their location was ascertainable: in the eighteenth century, Spanish priests had worked these veins to enormous profit, but they had been abandoned for years. Still another legendary example was the lost Naranjal mine, which was so prodigally rich its owner paved the path from his hacienda to the nearby church with bricks of pure silver. Gwin's stories went on and on, and Montholon's

The silent partner in Gwin's scheme to colonize Sonora was the Duc de Morny (left), the unscrupulous speculator and parliamentary leader who was Napoleon III's bastard half-brother and a recognized power behind the throne of the French Second Empire. (Of this dandy and libertine, a fellow politician remarked: "His life lacked austerity.") Morny pressed for intervention in Mexico, and with good reason: he stood to make a fortune from back-room deals connected with the venture. When word of the entry of French troops into Mexico City reached Paris in the summer of 1863, Morny's imperial relative commemorated his victory by building a lavish but temporary pavilion (right) in the Place de la Concorde.

eyes glistened as the Doctor assured him that these sources of wealth could be tapped again. The Marquis left murmuring that exalted personages might be interested in so dazzling a prospect.

A few days later Doctor Gwin received a caller in the person of Count Mercier, who until recently had been Napoleon's minister to the United States and was now attached to the Foreign Office. Mercier was a staunch supporter of the Confederate cause, and he and Gwin were able to converse frankly; they had been friends in Washington. At Mercier's suggestion, Gwin outlined a plan for colonizing and opening up Sonora, one calculated to enrich both the French and Mexican governments and to prove highly profitable as well to the entrepreneurs in charge. The plan seemed to hold stupendous possibilities, and the Count left in a state of excitement. Shortly thereafter a gorgeously liveried lackey delivered at Number 55 Boulevard Malesherbes a gilt-edged card which invited Doctor Gwin to confer with the president of the Corps Législatif, the Duc de Morny.

Morny was not only Napoleon's illegitimate half-brother but the Emperor's most influential adviser, and was largely responsible for France's intervention in Mexico; it was a speculation from which he expected to reap millions. The boldest and least scrupulous speculator in Europe, Morny was credited with

being the brains of Louis Napoleon's Second Empire.

Gwin and Morny met in the Duke's library and took to each other at once. The interview was private and confidential, which suited them both. They shared a number of traits: both thought on a grand scale, and both were prepared to risk much when the odds seemed in their favor. They were men who united bold imagination with cold calculation—a rare and usually winning combination—and who temperamentally preferred to do business by backstairs jockeying.

Gwin told Morny that the prestige of his reputation in California alone would attract thousands of miners to Sonora—the kind of rough, hardy men who would stop at nothing to get gold. After them would come farmers, merchants, artisans, educators—many of them, presumably, with Confederate leanings—and, as in California, cities, towns, and a framework of government would be created. Naturally those who got in on the ground floor would benefit most; but Gwin need hardly have pointed this out to so shrewd an operator as the Duc de Morny.

There was, however, one prerequisite which France alone could provide, and luckily she could provide it easily: military protection for the first emigrants against the bitterly hostile Indians. As soon as colonists arrived in sufficient numbers, they could defend themselves and the Indian problem would cease. Thus, if

7

the French army in Mexico would provide the necessary initial assistance, Gwin was prepared to promote a large-scale colonization effort.

Shortly after his interview with Morny, Doctor Gwin was summoned to an audience with the Emperor himself. He found Napoleon III poring over geological maps of Mexico. The Emperor's English was probably better than his French (brought up in Germany and Switzerland, he spoke both tongues with a thick German accent), and he responded eagerly to Gwin's proposals. Maximilian had to be consulted, of course, and he happened to be in Paris. A meeting was arranged, at which the Archduke listened to the American's proposals graciously and gave hearty encouragement.

It was now September, 1863. For Maximilian's further consideration, Gwin embodied his plan in a memorandum that read like a draft on the Bank of Golconda. Being a supple politician, the Doctor knew exactly how to appeal to the Archduke's vanity, his highmindedness, and his self-interest all at once. The memorandum spoke of "mines of fabulous richness— especially of silver" that had been worked in Spanish times. "One mine," Gwin specified, ". . . produced a solid piece of silver of the value of $4,700, which was sent as a present to the King of Spain. I cannot trust my memory to give the full details, and I have only my memory to rely upon, as the authorities and data of my researches were destroyed, with my whole Congressional library of about 2,000 volumes, at my plantation on the Mississippi River, by the army of General Grant during the siege of Vicksburg." But he was certain the Mexican archives would bear out everything he said; and in this he was on solid ground.

Maximilian was apparently dazzled, and on January 5, 1864, Gwin addressed a letter to Napoleon, formally soliciting military assistance. The Doctor also cautiously uncovered an aspect of the venture which hitherto had not been stressed, and which bore upon Napoleon's position in the game of power politics he was playing. If the North succeeded in suppressing the Rebellion, it would be in a position to send an army of formidable strength and high morale to expel the French—and probably Maximilian with them. Acting in concert with Great Britain, Napoleon had pledged to observe strict neutrality in the American conflict; secretly he favored the Confederates and was covertly aiding them, for he regarded the Richmond government as a probable future ally. Gwin understood the explosive elements in the situation, and he offered Napoleon a means of insurance against a future Yankee attack. He did not belabor the issue, but merely pointed out the desirability of having Sonora, which borders on the United

States, peopled with settlers who could be relied upon to defend their homesteads against any sudden thrust. Such a population in Sonora, Gwin observed, would present "an impregnable barrier to hostile attacks upon that portion of the Empire."

The growing tension in his relations with Washington was giving Napoleon some uneasy moments, and the notion of that "impregnable barrier" of tough fighting men appealed to him—especially since many of them were likely to be pro-Confederate. The Emperor graciously signified that he was considering the plan. But, cautious and secretive by nature, Napoleon let the matter drift until March, when Gwin applied pressure by a second memorandum, which contained phrases that would have caused the eyebrows of Secretary of State Seward to shoot upward in startled concern.

"Let the Civil War in the United States cease," Gwin had written, "and thousands of discharged soldiers, inured to hardship and camp life, and who will not go back to their former homes if they can help it, would overrun the country, subdue the Indians, and hold it against any force Mexico could bring into the field to expel them. This is the main reason why it should be occupied now . . ."

The thought of a horde of American adventurers, northern or southern, swarming into Sonora and appropriating those wonderful mines for themselves, with neither Napoleon nor Maximilian benefiting, was a horrid prospect, and the French Emperor was stirred to action. Gwin's proposals were laid before his cabinet; there, article by article, they were debated in the Emperor's presence, and article by article, they were approved.

Meanwhile, Morny and Gwin had reached a private arrangement between themselves whereby Morny became Gwin's silent partner. The Duke agreed to provide the capital not only to work the mines but to set up railroads, steamship lines, banks, and other commercial ventures as rapidly as Sonora was populated.

On April 14, 1864, with pomp and misgiving, Maximilian and his consort, Carlota, daughter of the King of the Belgians, set sail from their Adriatic dream villa, Miramar, for their new world. Two weeks later Doctor Gwin quitted Paris for England, where he was to take ship for Veracruz. With him went an autograph letter from Napoleon to General Achille Bazaine, commanding the French army of occupation in Mexico, ordering Bazaine to supply all necessary military assistance to put Gwin's plan into effect. The outlook could not have been brighter, and at the Tuileries it was whispered that upon his return, if the enterprise proved a success, Doctor Gwin might expect to receive a title. "Duke of Sonora" seemed fitting. The American news-

TEXT CONTINUED ON PAGE 83
A PORTFOLIO OF ILLUSTRATIONS CONTINUES ON THE FOLLOWING PAGES

8

Maximilian In Mexico

LIC. ANTONIO ARRIAGA COLLECTION, MEXICO, D.F.

Maximilian and Carlota—the faces of the Austrian archduke and his wife, the Belgian princess, seem to belong to the romantic leads of a light opera about some mythical Middle European principality. But because they allowed themselves to become the tools of a dictator's grab for empire, their story turned out to be Graustark with a cruel twist. The attempt to place Maximilian on the throne of Mexico was the improbable handiwork of the self-made Emperor of France, Napoleon III. Part genius, part mountebank, whose most notable monument was the superficial glitter of the Second Empire, he saw an opportunity for national aggrandizement that might assure him a fame equal to

IMPERIAL ARMS OF MEXICO, MUSEUM OF HISTORY, CHAPULTEPEC

that of his uncle, the great Bonaparte. Two circumstances prompted his undertaking. The first was a civil war in Mexico (1858–61), which had left the country in a state of anarchy and the bankrupt republican regime of Benito Juárez deeply in debt to European creditors—a perfect set-up for outside intervention. The second, of course, was the War Between the States; as long as it lasted, Napoleon knew, he could expect no interference. And so, in 1861, he set in train the events that were to bring Maximilian and Carlota to Mexico. Rarely has foreign meddling in the affairs of the Western hemisphere been so blatant—or its potential threat to the interests of the United States so great.

Like so many dictators before and since, Napoleon III (left) attempted to dazzle away problems at home by spectacular feats abroad; to him, the benefits of a French conquest of Mexico seemed almost limitless. But the responsibility was not his alone, for most of the monarchs of Europe were involved, either actively or because of close family ties. Ironically, had it not been for the Emperor's weakness for women, the whole shabby adventure might never have taken place. To compensate his wife, Eugénie, for his extramarital affairs, Napoleon allowed her to dabble in politics. (At right, in Franz X. Winterhalter's painting, the Empress—a coronet of flowers in her hair and a blue bow at her bodice—sits among her ladies-in-waiting.) Eugénie proceeded to become involved with a weird assortment of Mexican expatriates—malcontents, monarchists, and banished clericals—who were trying to bring about European intervention in the affairs of their troubled country. Soon Napoleon was swept up in their machinations, and a grand design began to form in his mind—the establishment of a puppet empire in Mexico and Central America. His pretext for this undertaking was a somewhat questionable list of damages to French property incurred during the recent civil war in Mexico. The governments of England's Queen Victoria and Spain's Queen Isabella II had similar claims, and in October, 1861, the three powers agreed to a joint occupation of Veracruz (with the backing of Pope Pius IX, who sought the return of church lands confiscated by the Juárez government). Meanwhile Napoleon had begun to search for a suitable candidate for the Mexican throne. His choice was the Archduke Maximilian, whose brother was Emperor Franz Josef of Austria and whose wife, Carlota, was the daughter of King Leopold of Belgium. Maximilian finally agreed—on the condition that the Mexicans offer him the crown by popular acclaim.

A Royal Affair

King Leopold I

Queen Victoria

Emperor Franz Josef

Queen Isabella II

Pope Pius IX

LIC. ANTONIO ARRIAGA COLLECTION, MEXICO, D.F.

CHATEAU DE VERSAILLES

12

A Hitch in Plans and a Staged Entrance

At Veracruz in the winter of 1861–62, it soon became apparent that the French had not come merely to seize customs duties from the republican regime of President Juárez. Realizing that they had been duped by Napoleon, the British and Spanish departed; the French proceeded to march against Mexico City. On May 5, at Puebla, they met a force of juarista irregulars and were repulsed with heavy losses: the lithograph at left shows the futile attempt of the 2nd Zouaves to reach the main Mexican position, Fort Guadalupe. "We have no partisans here . . . ," the French commander reported, "I have not met a single proponent of monarchy." Napoleon's reaction was to dispatch 30,000 more troops—and this time the ragged forces of the Mexican Republic were no match for the French. In May, 1863, Puebla fell after a two months' siege; a few days later Juárez fled Mexico City, and on June 7, the vanguard of Napoleon's army entered the capital. The painting below depicts the reception of General Achille Bazaine (right center, on a white horse) by monarchist sympathizers. A more elaborate welcome was staged later; spectators were provided with flowers to toss, and with free liquor. In the following months the French forces continued to win victories; they conducted rigged plebiscites and, to no one's great surprise, Maximilian was elected Emperor.

With crowds cheering and bandsmen blaring the just-composed Mexican imperial anthem, Maximilian and Carlota departed from their Adriatic palace, Miramar, on April 14, 1864. In the woodcut above, based on an eyewitness drawing, the royal couple are rowed out to a waiting escort of warships. As he entered the launch, the new Emperor of Mexico momentarily lost his composure. "Look at poor Max!" his wife exclaimed. "How he is weeping!" Below, a Viennese lithograph portrays the landing of Maximilian and Carlota at Veracruz. The ovation was entirely imaginary: no festive throngs turned out, and as the young monarchs drove nervously through deserted streets, it was the Empress who struggled to fight back her tears.

TWO
COUPLES,
TWO
MEXICOS

While Maximilian proceeded toward Mexico City, the President of the Republic of Mexico, Benito Juárez (shown here with his wife, Margarita) was making a desperate attempt to hold together the remnants of a government and an army in the deserts of the north. A pure-blooded Zapotec Indian, this small, dark-skinned man in his worn black suit became the symbol of his country's resistance to alien rule. When Maximilian innocently solicited his help, Juárez replied with characteristic eloquence. "It is given a man, sir," wrote the President to the Emperor, "to attack the rights of others, seize their goods, assault the lives of those who defend their nationality, make of their virtues crimes, and one's own vices a virtue, but there is one thing beyond the reach of such perversity: the tremendous judgment of history."

Maximilian, here adorned in his imperial ermine, regarded himself not only as the honest choice of his adopted people but as their ordained redeemer. He made an effort to mix with them, ate Mexican food and affected Mexican dress, and spoke always of "we Mexicans." An irresolute dreamer who professed liberal attitudes, he preoccupied himself with the drafting of unenforceable laws, the projection of impossible reforms, and the compilation of a manual of court etiquette which he pronounced "the most finished piece of work" on the subject ever written.

Strong-willed and ambitious, Carlota had pushed the husband she adored into a role for which he was supremely unsuited. As time went on, strains developed between them that were not eased by her increasingly neurotic behavior or her failure to produce an heir. If Carlota shared Maximilian's hopes, she also saw the pitfalls ahead. "There is room for a monarchy in this country," she wrote, "but none the less . . . this remains a gigantic experiment, for one has to struggle against the desert, the distance, the roads, and the most utter chaos."

17

LIC. F. A. SCHROEDER COLLECTION, MEXICO, D.F.

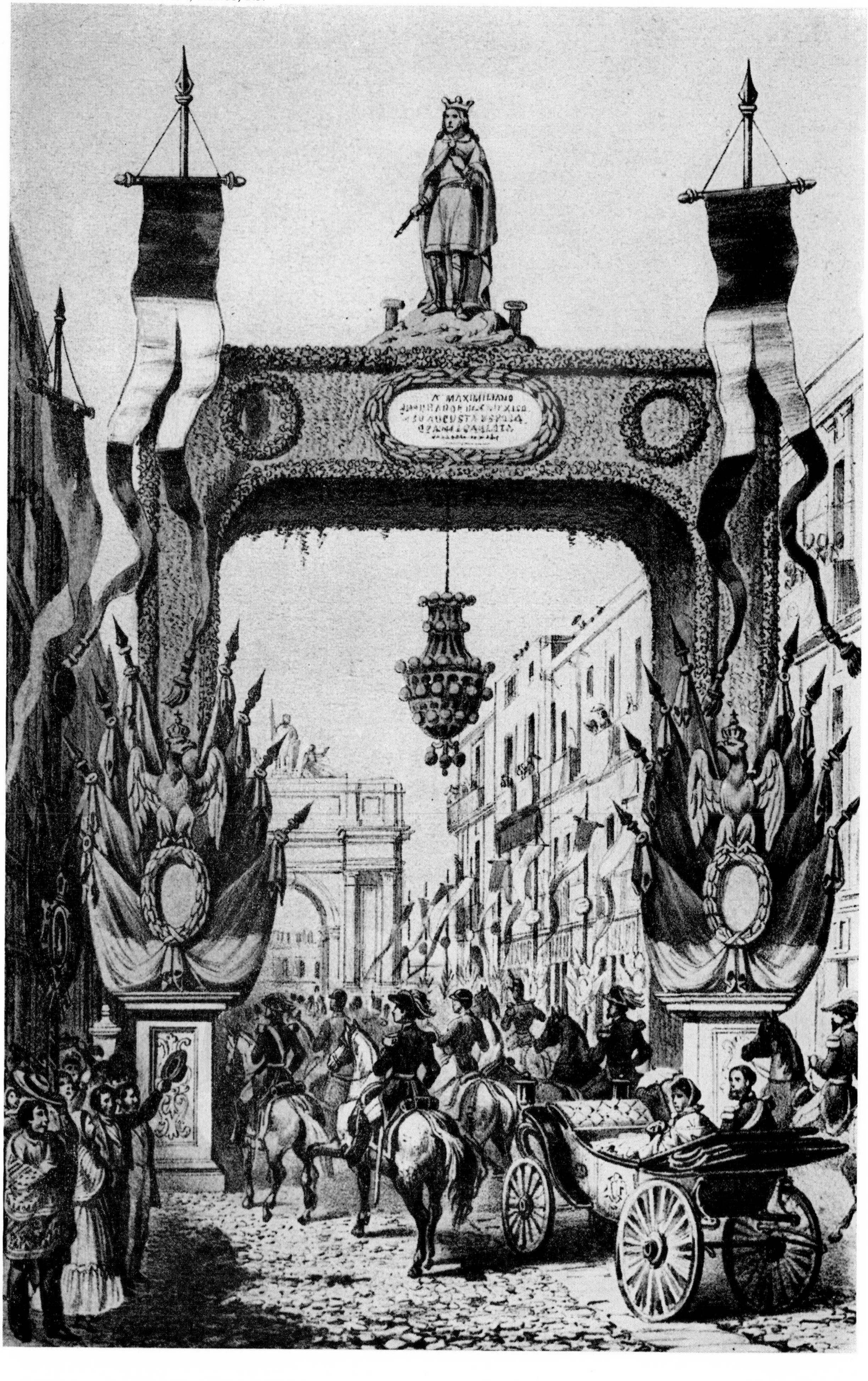

An Uneasy Crown

On June 12, 1864, the Hapsburg rulers reached Mexico City
and paraded in an open carriage under triumphal arches
like the one at left. (These had been erected in fantastic
numbers along the route from Veracruz—in one stretch of
some ten miles, there were 770 of them.) Conducted to the
National Palace, Maximilian and Carlota found their apartments overrun by vermin; it is said that the Emperor spent
the first night in his capital sleeping on a billiard table.
Later, they moved to a beautiful Spanish colonial castle in
nearby Chapultepec, where they set up housekeeping in
lavish style. During the first six months of his reign, Maximilian gave seventy lunches, twenty banquets, sixteen balls,
and twelve receptions; his wine bill alone was over $100,000.
But it was a life of uneasy luxury, for the war was never far
away. Guerrilla bands roamed at will, sometimes raiding
within the limits of the capital. In the encounters recorded
here, chinacos—as they were popularly known—skirmish with
Zouaves (above), attack a rear-guard detachment of the
French army (center right), and ambush a stagecoach (bottom right) carrying one of General Bazaine's couriers.

L'Illustration, JULY, 1863

L'Illustration, FEBRUARY 27, 1864

COLLAPSE OF AN EMPIRE

The prospects of Napoleon's puppet regime in North America were probably never bright to begin with; after April, 1865, they were hopeless. The French Emperor had gambled on a Confederate victory, and Appomattox had proved the end of more than one dream. The victorious North began to pressure the French relentlessly; the song sheet at left could not have expressed our government's position better. In a series of blunt notes, Secretary of State Seward called for the immediate evacuation of the French. Meanwhile, General Grant had massed 100,000 men under the command of General Phil Sheridan on the Rio Grande border. Napoleon had no desire to risk a war, and in January of 1866 he informed Maximilian that he had ordered the gradual withdrawal from Mexico of his expeditionary force. By fall, Maximilian was ready to abdicate. He shipped his baggage to Veracruz, went off to Orizaba to collect butterflies for six weeks—and changed his mind about leaving. On February 5, 1867, the French finally left Mexico City—an event depicted above—as the Emperor hid behind a curtain to watch them march away. He seemed almost relieved to see them go. As the French pulled out, the reborn armies of Juárez closed in. In April, Puebla was taken by a man who would one day be dictator of Mexico, General Porfirio Díaz. The painting at right, by a participant, shows Díaz (center, wielding a sword) entering the town.

"SOVEREIGN
OF THE
UNIVERSE"

Maximilian's last, forlorn hope was to fight on with the few native troops who still remained loyal to him. But as usual, indecision prevailed. His tiny army was caught and besieged at the town of Querétaro and the Emperor taken prisoner. Juárez was determined that foreign interventionists should be taught a lesson: on June 19, 1867, Maximilian and two of his Mexican generals went before a firing squad. ("What a glorious day!" he said, as he emerged from his prison cell. "I have always wanted to die on just such a day.") When word of the execution reached Paris, Edouard Manet did the painting at left— which the French government forbade him to exhibit. If Manet was a vastly talented artist, he was no historian: Maximilian did not stand in the middle (that honor he

gallantly accorded to one of the generals), nor did he wear a sombrero. The following January an Austrian naval vessel brought his body back from Mexico, and when the coffin arrived at the Adriatic port of Trieste, a magnificent funeral barge (above) was waiting. One last footnote might be added to this tragic saga. In the summer of 1866, Carlota had travelled to Paris in the hope of persuading Napoleon to postpone the evacuation of the French army. He had wept—and promised her nothing. Under the weight of misfortune, her mind snapped. Though she lived until 1927, sixty years after the demise of her husband, she never regained her sanity. To the very end, Carlota spoke of him as the "Sovereign of the Universe."

23

In the summer of 1915, 1,300 blue bloods played soldier for thirty days at Plattsburg. A bully time was had by all— even though it was a far cry from the real thing

By FRANCIS RUSSELL

When Gentlemen Prepared for War

Few recall now those Plattsburg training camps of 1915 and 1916 where, during the dog days of late summer, several thousand sweaty, earnest businessmen-volunteers in unaccustomed khaki learned the manual of arms and how to form fours at a sleepy army post on the shores of Lake Champlain. The memory of their amateur soldiering—existing still in the minds of a few elderly men—has been obscured and overlaid by the mass levies of three intervening wars. Yet the Plattsburg idea was, for all its naïveté, the beginning in the United States of the twentieth-century conception of the citizen-soldier, the genesis of the officers' training camps of the two World Wars, a psychological preparation for the drafts that were to follow.

Until 1914 the Plattsburg idea was inconceivable. If there was one general reaction in the United States to the European war that broke out in mid-summer of that year, it was that Americans wanted to have no part in it. President Wilson appealed to his countrymen to be "impartial in thought as well as in action . . . neutral in fact as well as in name." Even ex-President Theodore Roosevelt, who never believed in keeping his belligerency under a bushel, felt at the outbreak that the United States should remain entirely neutral.

The invasion of Belgium soon made impartiality of thought impossible. To most Americans the complicated military and diplomatic issues involved reduced themselves to the simple imagery of *Punch*'s cartoon showing Belgium as a small boy, stick in hand, defiantly blocking the pasture gate against a cudgel-swinging German. Other circumstances soon turned American sympathy toward the Allies—the ties of English language and literature, the Anglomania of the upper-class East, Allied skill and German ineptness in

This Plattsburg rookie wrestling with the intricacies of an army field cot is Percy Haughton, the famed coach of a Harvard football team that had gone undefeated for three years.

propaganda. Sympathy for the Allies, however, was a far cry from any wish to join the slaughter. Even after the torpedoing of the *Lusitania* in May, 1915—probably the crucial incident that determined the entry of the United States—Wilson could still be re-elected on the slogan: "He kept us out of war!"

A few American leaders felt from the war's outbreak that United States participation was inevitable. Most outstanding and authoritative of these was the Army's Commander of the Department of the East and former Chief of Staff, Major General Leonard Wood. For years Wood had been preaching preparedness to an indifferent public and an uninterested government. And to his dismay, as the millions mobilized in Europe, the strength—if one could call it that—of the United States Army was only 80,000 men.

Wood—without whose zeal the Plattsburg idea would never have taken form—was not only the Army's senior general but its outstanding one. His career was extraordinary in that he had come to the Army from Harvard Medical School rather than the generals' way, from West Point. As a young medical lieutenant he had first served in Arizona with an army detachment that captured Geronimo and ended the Apache War. During this campaign he had shown so much courage, military skill, and readiness to take command in emergencies that he was awarded the Medal of Honor. He did not get a chance to prove this capacity on a more expanded stage, however, until the Spanish-American War. Although only a medical captain at the outset, he was soon appointed colonel of one of the three volunteer regiments of frontiersmen—the Rough Rider Regiment—with his friend Theodore Roosevelt as second-in-command. It was like releasing a powerful spring. By the end of the war Wood's energy and ability had made him a major general of volunteers.

Subsequently, while military governor of Cuba's Santiago City and then of Santiago Province, he ruled

Bankers, merchants, lawyers, public officials, heroes of the gridiron, and squires of the fox hunt—the original Plattsburg recruits were a carefully chosen lot whose antecedents were likely to be Ivy League and eastern seaboard aristocracy. During the month that the "millionaire rookies" (as the newspapers were fond of calling them) trained at the camp on Lake Champlain, their progress was carefully watched by General Leonard Wood (left), the man responsible for this experiment in preparedness. Shown from left, counterclockwise, are some typical Plattsburgers. The two men standing for inspection are a onetime Harvard football captain, Hamilton Fish, Jr., (who, ironically, would become an isolationist congressman before the Second World War) and the ex-Governor of Puerto Rico, Regis H. Post. Below, two recruits—J. D. Milburn and Van S. Merle Smith—pose with a machine gun; and a former New York police commissioner, Rhinelander Waldo (seated, left), looks on as Company E receives instructions. The young man standing guard duty is another future congressman, Robert L. Bacon, Jr., whose father was once ambassador to France. Above him: Theodore Roosevelt's youngest son, Quentin, who would die in France in 1918. At Wood's invitation, T. R. visited Plattsburg; speaking before the assembled camp (opposite), he violently attacked President Wilson's efforts to preserve neutrality.

as America's first proconsul, showing himself a brilliant administrator. He became as popular with Cubans as he was with his own men. In 1899, President McKinley appointed him military governor of the whole island, and some months later raised him to the permanent rank of brigadier general. No such rapid advance by a nonprofessional had ever before been known in the Regular Army. His success in Cuba was followed by equal success in the Philippines, where he became governor of the Moro Province and, in 1906, Commanding General of the Philippines Division. In 1908, he returned to the United States to take command of the Department of the East. In the spring of 1910 he was appointed Chief of Staff and ranking officer of the army he had joined twenty-five years before as a contract surgeon. He was to hold the post until 1914.

With his imperious yet somehow gentle face and proud, hawk nose, Wood looked every inch the general, from his chain spurs to the dog-headed riding crop that he always carried with him and that became his identity tag. There was no bombast about him, nothing of the martinet; he did not need to assert an authority that was innate. What has been said falsely of many generals could be said truly of him: he was loved by his men.

It was in Germany in 1902 that he began to reflect on the need for American preparedness, when, as a military observer, he stood beside the Kaiser and watched the field maneuvers of the German Army. That magnificently formidable machine might some

day become a threat to the world, as his fellow observer, the old English marshal Lord Roberts, remarked to him. But Wood knew the absurd impos-
sibility of trying to create any American equivalent.
What he conceived of was the formation of a citizen
army, a vast, trained reserve on the Swiss model, mili-
tarily efficient yet not militaristic.

For years he tried to make his laggard countrymen
aware of the need of increased national defense. He
talked preparedness night and day. He wrote articles
and gave interviews. He spoke to clubs and colleges all
over the country. He encouraged the formation of preparedness groups like the National Security League
and the American Defense Society. When clouds were
gathering over Mexico in 1913, and German officers
in their messes were drinking toasts to the Day, Wood
took a first practical step by setting up two small summer camps for college students. Through such camps,
he felt, young men would not only receive an introduction to army life, but—more importantly—would
become concerned with the problem of national defense.

At Gettysburg, Pennsylvania, and Monterey, California, 222 students from ninety colleges spent five
weeks at their own expense, drilling, parading, firing
on the range, and finally—after a sham battle lasting
a week—making a sixty-five-mile forced march. The
camps were endorsed by educators as well-known as
ex-President Eliot and President Lowell of Harvard,
President Hibben of Princeton, and President Hadley

of Yale. Even the pacific Wilson gave his approval. In
1914 three times as many students enrolled, and additional camps were held at Ludington, Michigan; Ashe-
ville, North Carolina; and Burlington, Vermont.

By the time of the sinking of the *Lusitania* most
Americans had begun to reconcile themselves to the
need for increased military preparedness, and an artic-
ulate minority demanded the entry of the United
States on the side of the Allies. Sternly voluble spokesman for the war hawks was Theodore Roosevelt, who
felt that after the loss of so many American lives on
the *Lusitania* it was "inconceivable we should refrain
from action." Increasing numbers of venturesome
Americans had drifted north to join the Canadian
Army. Others like Henry Beston, Robert Hillyer, and
John Dos Passos were paying their passage across the
ocean to serve as volunteer ambulance drivers with
the French.

Two days after the *Lusitania* went down, a group
of fifteen romantically indignant young Harvard grad-
uates—among them Theodore Roosevelt, Jr., Hamilton
Fish, Jr., Elihu Root, Jr., and Robert Bacon, Jr., son
of the former U.S. Ambassador to France—met in New
York and sent a telegram to President Wilson demand-
ing that adequate military measures, "however serious," be taken. But Wilson, engaged in dispatching
notes to the Imperial German Government, still did
not consider preparedness a pressing question. Young
Ted Roosevelt and two others then approached General Wood to ask if he would hold a summer camp,

CONTINUED ON PAGE 89

27

FACES FROM THE PAST—XIV

Seventy-one years after the murders, doubt persists, and if you were to ask, "Was she guilty?" the chances are a good twenty-to-one that the answer would be affirmative. The law may protect a defendant from double jeopardy, but it cannot prevent the public from passing judgment. What might be called the public's "case" against the rather plain young woman began long before the Commonwealth of Massachusetts brought her to trial. It commenced, in fact, the day after the bodies of her father and stepmother were found. Rumor and half-truth spread like wildfire, feeding on the smouldering flames of fear, creating almost overnight a legend that has never disappeared. The story, as it began to build during those first hours, went something like this: On the hot, humid morning of August 4, 1892, in an angular frame house on Second Street, in Fall River, Massachusetts, Mrs. Andrew Borden was brutally hacked to death by someone wielding a hatchet or an axe. Somewhat later, in another room of the house, her husband was similarly dispatched. The news that a respectable couple had been murdered in their own home in broad daylight brought the town's normal activities to a standstill; two hours after the crime was discovered, thousands of hot, angry people were milling about in Second Street, muttering, questioning, venturing opinions, wondering where the mad killer would strike next, who the next victim would be. Before nightfall the town's newspapers had taken over the case, describing the murder scenes in all their gory detail and hinting broadly at suspects.

Now, almost any news about Andrew Borden would have been enough to make the mill town sit up and take notice; he was a silent, sour man who had made money as an undertaker and as exclusive agent for Crane's Patent Casket Burial Cases, who was now an extremely well-to-do banker and real estate owner. It was common gossip that neither of his daughters, Emma or Lizzie, got on well with their stepmother, whom Borden had married twenty-seven years earlier. But Emma, it seemed, was out of town when the murders were committed. Lizzie had found her father's body on the sitting-room couch and sent the hired girl, Bridget, for help; a little later Bridget and a neighbor discovered Mrs. Borden in the upstairs guest room, lying face down in a pool of blood. So suspicion soon fastened upon the thirty-two-year-old Lizzie, a slight, ordinary-looking girl with brown hair and a habit of saying just what was in her mind.

First Lizzie had killed her stepmother, townsfolk said; then, after cleaning her hands and clothes, she had busied herself about the house for an hour and a half, sewing, ironing, reading a magazine, waiting for her father to return from downtown. After he came in, stretched out on the couch, and dozed off, she attacked him with the same weapon she had used on Mrs. Borden. Again she removed the blood from her clothes and from the axe (all within the space of ten minutes, and so effectively that later chemical tests revealed no trace of it), then called for help. Someone said she never shed a tear when the bodies were discovered; the maid Bridget was said to have heard her laugh coldly when her father entered the house; there was talk that she had tried to buy poison the day before the murders; someone said she was seen burning a dress afterward.

Five days after the crime an inquest was held; two days later Lizzie Borden was arrested and held without bail pending trial. Meanwhile the wildest theories and rumors gained currency. But most damning of all was the verse—those unforgettable four lines of doggerel, sung to the tune of "Ta-ra-ra-boom-de-ay," which condemned her forever in the public mind, no matter what any court might decide:

> Lizzie Borden took an axe
> And gave her mother forty whacks;
> When she saw what she had done
> She gave her father forty-one.

In June, 1893, the trial opened in New Bedford, and for thirteen days the jury heard a great deal of conflicting testimony (much of it highly embarrassing to the prosecution), and witnessed a brilliant performance by the defense attorney. One of the most telling accusations made by the prosecution was that Lizzie had not been in the barn behind the house between 11:00 and 11:15 on the fatal morning, as she claimed—that she had, in fact, been bludgeoning her father to death at that very moment. A sensation of the trial was a surprise witness for the defense, an ice-cream peddler who maintained stoutly and credibly that he had seen a woman, dressed as Lizzie purportedly was, emerging from the barn just when she said she had.

When the trial ended, the jurors were out for a little more than an hour before bringing in a verdict of "Not Guilty." Spectators in the courtroom applauded, and an editorial writer for the New York Sun summed up the trial: "A chain of circumstantial evidence is strong only if it is strong in every necessary link . . . The chain tested at New Bedford the past twelve days was proved fragile indeed, not merely at one place, but in almost every link."

Legally, the defendant was acquitted. Theoretically, her ordeal was over. But the public considered her guilty—guilty by innuendo, if nothing else. Not even her death in 1927 ended the trial of Lizzie Borden. Books and plays were written about her, eventually there were movies, a television show, a ballet. Finally, Edward D. Radin came to her defense with a fine book, *Lizzie Borden: The Untold Story*, that argues her innocence convincingly while revealing the falsehoods behind the legend. There the matter might rest at last, were it not for the cruel verse: "Lizzie Borden took an axe, and gave her mother forty whacks . . ."

—*Richard M. Ketchum*

If he had never come across the Great Sea, if he had never founded his peaceful commonwealth, we would still be in debt to William Penn. At twenty-six, with all his better-known achievements before him, he performed an enduring service to the liberties of the English-speaking world. It was London in 1670, ten years after the overthrow of Cromwell's Puritans and the Restoration of the Stuarts. A new crusading faith was making its appearance (they are always annoying to the authorities), and young Penn, a Quaker agitator, was on trial for disturbing the peace.

Members of the court threatened the jury with fines ment of his peers, or by the Laws of the land." Now that pledge, so painfully wrung from King John, was being discarded by the courts. Three years before Penn's trial, the House of Commons had investigated Lord Chief Justice Keeling in connection with official misconduct, asserting that he had undervalued, vilified, and condemned Magna Charta, "the great preserver of our lives, freedom and property"; and on November 13, 1667, an entry was made in the Parliament Journal: "Resolved that the precedents and practice of fining or imprisoning jurors for verdicts is illegal." But this resolution had not stopped the practices of the judges.

THE ORDEAL OF WILLIAM PENN

Long before he founded his Quaker commonwealth in America, he stood up for religious freedom against the awesome power of the Crown—and put the entire English-speaking world in his debt

By FRANCIS BIDDLE

and hinted at torture if they did not bring in a verdict to the judge's taste—but they would not yield: "NOR WILL WE EVER DO IT!" their foreman shouted in answer to Penn's impassioned appeal, "Give not away your right!" The trial is a landmark in English and American history.

Less than 300 years ago these twelve men established the independence of English juries: they should make their own decisions, and must not be "led by the nose" by any court. The right they defended was embodied in Magna Charta, which provided: "No Freeman shall be taken, or imprisoned, nor be disseized of his Freehold or Liberties or Free-Customs or be Outlawed or Exiled, or any other ways destroyed; nor we shall not pass upon him nor condemn him, but by lawful judg-

What did stop them was the obstinate courage of an English jury who had faith in *their* law, and knew how to assert it, under the skillful leadership of the man whom they were trying.

The members of this jury were little, everyday men, none of them gentlemen, as Penn was described in the indictment, men of no importance. In ordinary circumstances a trial for disturbing the peace would have been held before only a single judge, who would quickly have sent the accused to jail, and the case would have been forgotten. But Penn had fired the Quakers with his dogged insistence that they had the right to worship their own God in their own way; to doff their headgear to no man, not even to any judge, for to God only was such obeisance due; and to meet quietly to worship in the open air in Gracechurch Street (sometimes known as "Gracious Street"), in the parish of Bridgeward, London.

Penn was behind this "nuisance," and was causing all the trouble, claiming the rights of Englishmen—just as if Quakers could be thought of in those terms. So the Crown decided to put on a show; and summoned the Lord Mayor, Sir Samuel Starling, in his robes and his massive gold chain and his rather pitiful ignorance of the law, even if he could recognize a nuisance, especially when "rights" were being claimed to defend it. With him sat the Recorder, John Howel, the chief

And there was a goodly crowd of spectators who hated judges, and would not observe silence in court, and so strongly expressed their sympathy with the prisoners that now and then the Recorder had to call them to order.

. . . William's father, Sir William Penn, a Royalist at heart, was still a practical man and knew how to get along during the Protectorate. He advanced under Cromwell to become Rear Admiral of the Irish Seas and Vice Admiral in command of England's Third Fleet. After Sir William defeated the Dutch in 1652, when William was eight, the Protector appointed him

criminal judge of the City of London, equally unlearned in the law which he was supposed to administer, a stupid man with little to sustain him except a few worn-thin Latin proverbs which he took delight in misapplying. He was a dull, heavy man, who was soon angry when the trial came alive, and kept his hot temper simmering; he suspected that Penn was making fun of him—which indeed Penn was. Sir John Robinson, the prosecutor for the Crown, was Lieutenant of the Tower and had come to know this obstinate young Quaker agitator and pamphleteer when he had been sent to the Tower for nine months not long before to keep him out of mischief—"in safe custody," as the phrase went. Four aldermen also sat on the bench, all of them knights, and three knighted sheriffs.

General at Sea; many enemy ships, casualties, prisoners, and prizes lay to his credit. But in two or three years the Admiral was in the Tower, suspected of being too close to the exiled Charles II. Released in five weeks, he went to his castle at Macroon in Ireland, and it was there that William saw the "inner light" for the first time—the quickening of man's soul by direct mystical communication with its Creator. For, as we are informed by various Penn biographers, an itinerant and eloquent Quaker named Thomas Loe had been invited to Macroon, and when he preached, a black servant belonging to William's father wept aloud; William, watching his father with awe, saw the tears running down his cheeks, and he too was deeply moved. They were told of the new doctrine that men had the right to wait upon the Lord unaided by any kind of priest. Loe talked of the simplicity of honest, plain living, devoid of plumes and laces, and of the dignity of humility.

The Penns lived four years in Ireland. Oliver Cromwell died in 1658, when William was fourteen. "It was the joyfullest funerall that I ever saw," wrote the essayist and diarist, John Evelyn, "for there was none that Cried, but dogs, which the souldiers hooted away with a barbarous noise, drinking & taking tabacco in the streetes as they went." The Penns had returned from Ireland by 1660, when Charles II entered London in triumph, and the boy may have seen "the wayes strew'd with flowers, the bells ringing, the streetes

chapel. For this beginning of nonconformity at the age of seventeen, Penn was finally expelled.

Samuel Pepys professed to be a friend of the Admiral, and though he could write in his diary: "Had Sir W. Pen, who I hate with all my heart . . . and his son, William . . . to dinner," the two were boon companions. Pepys found Penn "sociable, able, cunning" and full "of merry discourse," fond of gaudy dress and lewd plays. Sir William taught Pepys to take good drafts of sack in the morning to cure headaches caused by too much drinking the night before. We must take Pepys with a generous pinch of salt, but there is enough in this brief description to indicate the gulf between the father, with his genial sensuality, and the

ILLUSTRATED FOR AMERICAN HERITAGE BY MICHAEL BIDDLE

hung with tapissry, fountaines running with wine." Admiral Penn, who had helped in the Restoration, was knighted and made a Navy commissioner, with juicy emoluments in the form of commissions on purchases, which added to his already large landed fortune.

That same year William was sent to Christ Church College at Oxford and entered as a "gentleman commoner." His experience there was brief. He was shocked by the "Hellish Darkness and Debauchery" of the place, which was happily pro-Royalist. The persecution of the Puritan sects had already begun. His friend Thomas Loe was in jail in Oxford for teaching the Quaker faith; but John Owen, a famous Puritan preacher, dismissed as dean of Christ Church when the Restoration came, was exhorting nonconforming students, Penn among them, in the Puritan tradition. They refused to wear surplices and would not go to

son, disgusted at the dissipation of Oxford. Apparently about this time there arose a severe misunderstanding between the two. William said that his father had administered him "bitter usage," whipping, beating, and turning him out of doors. The Admiral found a letter of Dr. Owen's to his son. Outraged but puzzled, he took it to Pepys, who thought that the Puritan preacher had "perverted" the boy, and now perceived what had put Sir William "so long off the hookes."

The father relented. He loved his son, but could not understand the lad's devotion to the Quakers, with their plain clothes and twaddle about the inner light. The Admiral was no mystic and knew he could do very much for his son if the boy would only let him. Forgiving him then, and changing his tactics, he sent William off to France with some persons of quality, among them Robert Spencer, later the Earl of Sunderland, who became William's lifelong friend. It was the summer of 1662; Penn was eighteen.

Penn wrote later that a man attacked him for not returning a salute and that he had disarmed his attacker but had not killed him. Instead of boasting, Penn philosophized, a bit solemnly, as was characteristic of his youth: "I ask any man of understanding or conscience if the whole ceremony were worth the life of a man, considering the dignity of the nature, and the importance of the life of man, both with respect to God, his Creator, himself, and the benefit of civil society?"

At the Académie Protestante de Saumur, Penn became a friend of the famous theologian and metaphysician Moïse Amyraut, the president of the college; lodged at his house; and imbibed his unflinching philosophy of toleration and religious liberty, learning in his classes to reject predestination and glory in personal liberty and to practice charity as well as piety.

Back in London in 1664 young Penn had become, according to Mrs. Pepys, "a most modish person, grown . . . a fine gentleman," with his athletic build and candid eyes. He studied law for a short time at Lincoln's Inn, and his curriculum included readings of Dryden and of Beaumont and Fletcher.

For a second time war was declared against Holland, and William joined his father for a few weeks on the *Royal Charles*. The Admiral, who had been made Great Captain Commander, sent his son as a personal messenger to the King, hoping that this would be the beginning of a brilliant career based on royal favor. From Harwich the boy wrote his father, whom he cherished: "I . . . firmly believe that if God has called you out to battle, He will cover your head in that smoky day . . . Your concerns are most dear to me. It's hard, meantime, to lose both a father and a friend." He had not yet made the choice between the kind of future his father wished for him and the way of life his instincts were reaching for, the way of the Quakers. He was moved by their persecutions and tortures— they would not meet in secret—and he saw dissenters in stocks, pelted and jeered at by the crowds.

The Great Plague had struck London. Lincoln's Inn, where Penn was again reading law, was deserted. Out of a population of half a million, nearly seventy thousand people died. Along the city's half-empty streets walked men to collect the corpses, crying, "Bring out your dead, bring out your dead!" Dr. Amyraut had said that man's responsibility to his brother was the ultimate morality, and Quakers worked to save the sick and helped carry out those who had died. Suffering increases nonconformity, and as unrest grew in the year of the Great Plague, the authorities took steps to suppress it. As usual, these

had the opposite effect. The Quaker Act three years before had made it unlawful for five or more Quakers to assemble "under pretense of worship." The same year the Act of Uniformity required clergymen to follow exactly the established Prayer Book. And now the Five Mile Act forbade any nonconformist preacher to come within five miles of a corporate town. This suppression caused Catholics, Quakers, and Independents to protest by active disobedience.

Sir William meanwhile was triumphant over the Dutch at the battle of Lowestoft, and in September, 1665, brought home a host of prizes. It was his last battle, and his health began to fail. He sent his son to Ireland to settle the estates which the King had given him. Serving under the Earl of Arran, young Penn helped restore order, and was praised for his works. In Cork he went to hear Thomas Loe speak at a Quaker meeting, was singularly affected, and realized then that his decision had been made: "It was at this time that the Lord visited me with a certain sound and testimony of His eternal word." He knew himself to be a "seeker," and began regularly to go to meetings of the Friends. But he still loved a good fight.

At one of the meetings a soldier came in to break up the group. Penn took him by the neck and started to throw him downstairs, but more soldiers came and arrested the Quakers. When the mayor saw Penn among them, he ordered him released, but Penn insisted he be treated like the others. He always practiced what he preached. Then he acted as lawyer for his fellow prisoners. On what charge had they been arrested, he asked? By way of answer they were all sent to jail. Penn protested to the Earl of Orrery and was released. His father, who had evidently heard of William's association with the Quakers, wrote him to come to see him in England without delay—"unless for necessary rest or refreshment" on the road. William returned with a fellow Quaker, Josiah Coale, who had been persecuted "and dragged bareheaded under the spouts in time of rain," and took him to visit his father, a gesture hardly calculated to effect a reconciliation. After Coale withdrew, his father burst out—did he have to use *thee* and *thou*? William must use *you* in speaking to older people or persons of high rank. But William, fortified by his brief taste of martyrdom, refused. Quakers, he said, recognized no rank. His father suggested that he uncover before the King, the Duke of York, *and* his father; but William, though he loved his father, would not. Exasperated, Sir William ordered his son from the house, saying he would dispose of his estates to those that pleased him better.

After this it was natural that William should throw himself without reserve into the Quaker cause, living

CONTINUED ON PAGE 104

A CHRONOLOGICAL CHART
OF THE
VISIONS OF DANIEL & JOHN.

The Trumpeter of Doomsday

By HAROLD A. LARRABEE

William Miller applied good Yankee arithmetic to
biblical prophecies and convinced thousands
that the hour of Christ's Second Coming was upon them

Opposite: In 1842 the Millerite leaders had 300 large (4'8" by 3'3") lithographs printed, to serve as visual aids for their lecturers. Mystifying without a key, the chart is actually an exposition of the biblical books of Daniel (left half) and Revelation (right half)—with special emphasis, of course, on the passages from which the Millerites derived their predictions of the Second Coming and the end of the world. The large human figure is the metal image of Nebuchadnezzar's dream (Daniel 2:31–45), interpreted by Daniel as symbolizing five future kingdoms of the earth, and by the Millerites, in retrospect, as symbolizing specifically Babylon, Media and Persia, Greece, Pagan Rome, and the "ten kingdoms" of the Germanic barbarians. The strange and horrifying beasts on both sides of the chart are those described in Daniel 7, and in Revelation 12 and 13, interpreted and captioned to suit the beliefs of the Millerites. The chart is roughly chronological from top to bottom, the numbers in large type being the dates and figures crucial to calculations that the infallible end would come in 1843. There were several ways of reaching this conclusion; two of the most important are shown just above the words "A Chronological Chart." Leviticus 26:23–24 speaks of the Lord punishing Israel "yet seven times for your sins"; considering each "time" as a prophetic year, or 360 ordinary years, the Millerites got 2,520 years; and subtracting from this 677 B.C.—the date at which it was assumed the Lord's punishment began—they got 1843. Or, starting with the statement in Daniel 8:14, "Unto two thousand and three hundred days [years]; then shall the sanctuary be cleansed," they subtracted 457 B.C., the date when, according to Miller's reading of Scripture, the desecration of the sanctuary (the earth) had begun. Again it came out, very satisfactorily, 1843. Q.E.D.

On October 22, 1844, thousands of Americans in widely scattered localities left their homes for what, they were perfectly convinced, would be the last time. Their leaders had meticulously corrected an earlier prediction that 1843 would be the final year. Now they were ready.

Many of them had given away or abandoned their property; some had let their crops go to ruin. They went in solemnly excited groups to meetinghouses and tabernacles to witness the Second Coming of Christ and the imminent destruction of the world. In the great moment now at hand, they fervently believed, they would "go up" to blissful eternal life, while millions of sinners and scoffers would be thenceforth doomed to the ineffable tortures of hell.

In an atmosphere increasingly strained they waited, looking for the first fearful sign of the Advent. The day wore on, while their leaders exhorted them to stay calm and assured them that the time of the Lord was indeed upon them. It was only a question of hours or minutes. Darkness fell. The hours passed, each more tense than the one before. Surely, they now felt, midnight must be the appointed instant. . . .

The man who was chiefly responsible for the mathematically precise expectations of these people was William Miller, of Low Hampton, New York, in the Champlain Valley—a plain, honest, self-educated farmer with a flair for arithmetic persuasively applied to what he believed to be literal and infallible premises. Everyone agreed that he was "a man mighty in the Scriptures," who always seemed to know what he was talking about. But the secret of his great success with his audiences, despite the fact that he was said to be slow of speech, was stated by Miller himself. "If you wish your people to *feel*," he said, "*feel yourself.*"

The intensity of Miller's feeling still clings to the words of one of his typical "Second Coming" exhortations:

The "official" portrait of Wil-
liam Miller, "published by per-
mission" in 1843, conveys some
sense of his utter self-assur-
ance in expounding the Book
of Daniel. Opposite: perhaps
it was the notable success of
Joshua V. Himes, Miller's
chief publicist, that prompted
anti-Millerites to such elab-
orate efforts as this satirical
broadside of 1844. Miller and
his famous chart "go up
triumphantly atop the Boston
tabernacle; but Parson Himes,
snagged by the Devil, remains
below among his moneybags

Ah! what means that noise? Can it be thunder? Too long—too loud and shrill—more like a thousand trumpets sounding an onset. It shakes the earth . . . See how it reels. How dreadful! How strange!

The very clouds are bright with glory . . . See, the heavens do shake, the vivid clouds, so full of fire, are driven apart by this last blast, and rolling up themselves, stand back aghast— And O, my soul, what do I see? A great white throne, and One upon it . . . Before him are thousands and thousands and thousands of wingèd seraphim, ready to do his will.

The last trumpet sounds—the earth now heaves a throb for the last time, and in this last great throe her bowels burst, and from her sprang a thousand thousand, and ten thousand times ten thousand immortal beings into active life . . . I saw them pass through the long vista of the parted cloud, and stand before the throne . . .

The air now became stagnated with heat; while the dismal howlings of those human beings who were left upon the earth, and the horrid yells of the damned spirits . . . filled my soul with horror not easily described.

It is hardly surprising to learn from a contemporary report that words such as these, uttered repeatedly in the 1830's, created "much excitement . . . a great breaking down, and much weeping" in places such as Montpelier, Vermont; or that in Lansingburgh, New York, "infidels, deists, Universalists and sectarians

were all chained to their seats in perfect silence for hours—yes, days—to hear the old, stammering man talk about the Second Coming of Christ, and show the manner, object, time, and signs of His Coming." Fire-and-brimstone preaching was nothing new in that part of the country. But the operative phrase which distinguished this revivalist from all his fellows was "the time and signs" of the Awful Last Day, for which he was prepared to furnish copious and resounding Bible proofs. He first announced the end of the world as fixed between March 21, 1843, and March 21, 1844. After the latter date had passed uneventfully, the prediction was revised to October 22, 1844. These rash prophecies set off one of the greatest mass delusions in American history; and the prophet's converts have been charged with a greater variety of ridiculous and fanatical acts than perhaps any religious group in modern times. Before the "crisis" years of 1843–44 were reached, Miller's followers must have numbered in the hundreds of thousands, most of whom, on that October night, were awaiting the Day of Judgment.

Miller was anything but a rabble-rouser at heart. The oldest of sixteen children, he was born in Pittsfield, Massachusetts, on February 15, 1782. When he was four years old, his father, Captain William Miller,

GRAND ASCENSION OF THE MILLER TABERNACLE!
Miller in his Glory, Saints and Sinners in one great CONGLOMERATION!

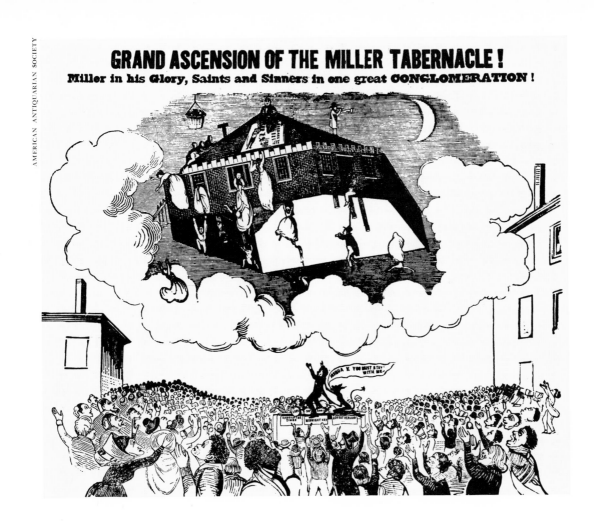

a veteran of the Revolution, moved to a farm in Low Hampton, New York, close to the Vermont line. The boy grew up in that small village, which afforded only about three months of schooling each winter. Books were scarce in the hard-working Baptist household, his father's whole library consisting of a Bible, a psalter, and an old hymnbook. Most of William's early reading was done in books he earned by wood-chopping. Later he was able to borrow volumes on ancient and modern history from more affluent neighbors.

At fifteen he began to keep a diary, and soon became known as the village ghost-writer (or "scribbler-general"), who provided not only letters but sometimes verses for his less literate fellows. On January 3, 1803, his journal records his engagement to marry Miss Lucy P. Smith of Poultney, Vermont, some six miles from Low Hampton. The wedding took place six months later, and they began farming in his wife's village. At Poultney, Miller was an inveterate frequenter of the town library, where he encountered for the first time the skeptical writers of the Enlightenment, such as Voltaire and Thomas Paine.

Perplexed by doubts about his previous beliefs, he soon became, like many others in the same period, a deist and scoffer at the fundamentalism in which

he had been reared. Unlike atheism, deism did not deny the existence of a Supreme Being, but portrayed Him as having refrained, after the creation, from any further interference in the orderly Newtonian processes of Nature. But to the orthodox clergy of the day, this was "an emanation of the Devil," one of the many varieties of heresy that constituted what they called "the Reign of Infidelity" in Vermont. As they saw it, along with dire events in Europe, such heresy portended "the last days" preceding the return of Christ to earth. That was the conclusion reached in 1811 by the Reverend Ethan Smith of Poultney in his *Dissertation on the Prophecies relative to Anti-christ and the Last Times,* in which he identified Napoleon as "the terrible head of the Roman beast," and predicted the end of the world in the year 1866.

For twelve years William Miller remained a deist, and yet an exemplary citizen, a fact which refuted the orthodox dogma equating infidelity with personal immorality. A Mason of advanced degree, he became town constable and, in 1809, deputy sheriff of the county. A year later he turned to the military life, first as a lieutenant in the militia, then as a captain in the Regular Army. In the ensuing War of 1812, he underwent his baptism of fire at the Battle of Platts-

CONTINUED ON PAGE 95

37

The nation's waterways, once crisscrossed by countless ferries, are now bridged or tunnelled, and all but a few of the romantic old surface shuttles are, alas, sounding their final whistles and bells

FAREWELL TO THE FERRY

Text by C. BRADFORD MITCHELL
Photographs by DAVID PLOWDEN

Like closing enemy pincers on a battle map, the unfinished steel of a new bridge across the Hudson River brackets the ferryboat *Orange* as she steams toward Newburgh from Beacon, New York, in the year-old photo above. The scene was due to be repeated for a few months more—with *Dutchess* or *Beacon,* as often as not, cast in the role of the encircled victim. Then, early last November the bridge ends joined, the three boats were sold, and ferrying on the Hudson north of Manhattan Island came to an end.

It was no tiny fragment of American enterprise and history which died that November day. During most of the century and a half since Fulton, and less formally for decades before, the Hudson had been cross-hatched from the Battery to Troy by ferry lines numbering in the dozens. Every city or town of consequence could claim, at one time or another, at least one ferry slip. But bridges and tunnels came, and multiplied. Each killed a ferry line, or three, or five. Now only two lines ply the Hudson proper, both taking commuters to lower Manhattan. Here, for a little longer, on borrowed time, ferryboat pilots can look down on the familiar rush-hour scene at the right.

Populous as it has been, though, the Hudson is only one of a thousand battle areas in a long, losing world war that began when some primitive engineer first bridged an unfordable water barrier. On hundreds of other rivers, bays, lakes, and straits, this war raged on into our lifetimes. Now, for most American waters, it is over.

What will be the last American ferryboat? An educated guess might say a very sizable vessel—really a ship—which will be finally idled when we learn to bridge the mouth of the Delaware, or tunnel the Bay of Fundy, or fly heavy highway traffic across Lake Michigan. But it could just as well be a cable-guided, hand-propelled scow where some dusty county road runs down to a backwoods riverbank. Such boats still exist, as if neither Fulton nor Diesel had been born. Whatever its size or shape, there is at least a chance that the last of all our ferries may be among the survivors pictured on the following pages.

Susquehanna Charon on the Falcon's *ramp*

This way to the Roaring Bull, *the* Falcon, *and a vanished century!*

Leaving the Delaware at Port Jervis, U.S. 209 slants 150 miles through the Pennsylvania coal country to dead-end at the Susquehanna. Here the motorist must turn right or left on Pa. 14—*unless* he wants to ferry. If so, a finger sign will take him to the plank landing-ramp of either *Falcon* or *Roaring Bull,* rough-and-ready sternwheelers with no family resemblance whatever to a Staten Island ferryboat or a Great Lakes car ferry. A quarter-hour will find him back in the twentieth century, on U.S. 11; but for the interval, if he can forget that steam has given way to internal combustion, he will have been in the rural America of 1864.

Equally unsophisticated, yet more of our time, is the ubiquitous cable ferry. With some adjustment of skyline but none of boat, the view opposite could be (but is not) the Ohio in Pennsylvania, the Willamette in Oregon, the Nanticoke in Delaware, or the Wabash in Indiana.

Roaring Bull *drives for the far shore beyond* Falcon's *sternwheel.*

Landing ramp raised, the Falcon *drifts near where road meets river.*

At the head of Lake Champlain the cable ferry Stanley B *aims an arrow of foam from Chipmans Point, Vt., to Wright, N.Y.*

OVERLEAF: *Leaving Barclay Street recently, against a skyline mostly younger than she,* Binghamton *of the Erie-Lackawanna ferry fleet wears funnel insignia symbolizing the last-ditch merger of two parallel railroad ferry lines.*

Above: *What appears to be a two-funnelled* Monitor *in search of a* Merrimack *is actually the midship section of the Wabash Railway's Detroit River freight car ferry* Manitowoc, *seen against the Detroit skyline. Built in 1926, she illustrates the unglamorous modern type of open-decked, screw-propelled car float which serves the Wabash and the Chesapeake & Ohio's Pere Marquette District at the busiest rail crossing of the Great Lakes system, between Windsor, Ontario, and Detroit, Michigan.*

Below: *Perhaps the best-known ferry service in the world is New York's city-owned Staten Island Ferry, which still takes commuters and sightseers on a 25-minute crossing of Upper New York Bay for a nickel fare.*

The city fleet, founded in 1905 after over 200 years of varied services from island ports by rowboats, sailboats, and steamers, numbered nine vessels at the start of 1964. These include the world's three largest harbor ferries: but to genuine ferryboat buffs the pride of the fleet is its trio of twin-stackers, Dongan Hills, Knickerbocker, *and* Tompkinsville, *launched when the century was less than thirty years old. Here,* Knickerbocker *vacates her Manhattan slip to make room for a newer boat, while the funnels of one of her sisters rise in the foreground. Governors Island is at upper left.*

The red-painted Staten Island ferries promise to be the last survivors of their species at New York; but the classic two-stackers are already doomed to be replaced in the near future by a diesel trio, now being built in Texas.

Above: *Eighty-eight and a half years is a good old age for a man; for a ferry it is phenomenal. Yet on last Dominion Day, July 1, 1963, the Canadian National Railways Detroit River car ferry* Huron *marked her eighty-eighth anniversary of international service on waters connecting Lakes Huron and Erie. She has long since outlived all of her contemporaries on the Great Lakes system—and probably anywhere else in the world. A propeller boat built in the age of paddles, she is even nine years older than her side-wheel running mate,* Lansdowne. *Yet both are in sturdy operating condition, with no hint of retirement.*

Huron *was built originally for the Sarnia-Port Huron crossing of the St. Clair River, at the foot of Lake Huron, but was put out of business there by a rail tunnel completed in 1891. Sixty-four years later, on the Windsor-Detroit run, another tunnel conspired with buses to deprive her and* Lansdowne *of the distinction of being the only river ferries to carry passenger trains. She still hauls her eleven freight cars per trip; but in deference to her age (and* Lansdowne's *sixteen-car capacity) she rates the title of "spare boat."*

Below: *The* Chief Wawatam *has dominated the Straits of Mackinac crossing since 1911, when she joined the service linking the railroads of Michigan's upper and lower peninsulas. Though less than five miles across, the Straits are in winter the most rugged of all American ferry routes, with windrow ice at times packed forty feet high. Icebreakers though they are, with reinforced hulls and bow propellers, its ferries have always faced the risk of being locked for days in ice jams. Large stocks of emergency provisions have had to be carried, especially before 1955, when the* Chief *and her sister boats ferried the Lake Superior Limited and other passenger trains.*

A dim point of light materializes out of the thick, wet dark, followed by red and green spots, then cabin and headlight glow, as Mary Murray, Staten Island "streamliner" of 1937, surges into her slip.

Above: *Last of the Hudson's "long ferries" was the New York Central run from Cortlandt Street, Manhattan, to the West Shore slips at Weehawken, N.J., four miles of skyline-watching to stir even the most hardened commuter. Here, Albany whistles farewell to the Singer Building, which had overseen her goings and comings for thirty-four years.* Right: *There is mesmerism about the wake streaming from under a screw ferry's broad stern apron; yet old-timers say its twisting confusion cannot match a paddler's wide, creamy, hissing path.*

Lantern on paint-cracked Ellis Island *pilot-house lighted millions of immigrants to the Promised Shore between 1904 and 1955.*

Above: *At Weehawken the New York Central's Cortlandt Street ferries met others which had made the three-quarter-mile crossing from Forty-second Street to deliver midtown commuters to West Shore trains. Both services ended March 24, 1959. This picture of a main-deck cabin on the Niagara tells why. At rush hours, her cabins and decks were crowded. In between, she carried large cargoes of exquisite geometrical shadow patterns, with an occasional reader for human interest. The Lincoln Tunnel had drained off vehicular traffic. West Shore passenger trains were themselves a burden the company ardently wished to lay down. The ferryboat way of life was a good one; but supposed economic imperatives, and the I.C.C., said it had to go. Right: Still-glowing brasswork is a not-imperishable memorial to the venerable Newburgh-Beacon ferry, and to all of its bridge-strangled predecessors.*

47

Fires cold, cabins and vehicle gangways empty, the double-ended steamboat Orange, *last of scores of ferryboats on the Hudson*

Only her fore and aft radar scanners imply, as the *Orange* sits in the lay-up berth at Beacon, that these are the 1960's, when ferries are an anachronism. But the loading ramps beyond her are now quiet, and the cars which once rolled down them are lined up to pay their bridge tolls.

For the *Orange* herself there may yet be a few years of answering engine-room bells added to the even fifty she has already put in. At the auction which saw her sisters sold for scrap, she was bid in for $2,850 by Myles Rosenthal, a consulting engineer for whom she had become a *femme fatale*. Late last fall, he and a group of friends fired up her coal-burning boilers and brought her down the Hudson to Jersey City, where he plans to refit her for charter trips. En route, her whistle defied the enemy by saluting every river town that had once had a ferry.

C. Bradford Mitchell is Director of Information for the American Merchant Marine Institute. David Plowden is a free-lance photographer whose main interest has been documenting vanishing American landmarks.

... ve the Holland Tunnel, awaits a buyer at Beacon, New York.

Abandoned Arthur Kill ferry slip at Elizabeth, N.J.

The Last Days
and Valiant Death
of Nathan Hale

Ever since he was executed by the British on the morning of September 22, 1776, the death of Nathan Hale has been recognized as one of the great moments of American patriotism. Some years ago the late George Dudley Seymour gathered all the contemporary descriptions of the young hero's career that he could find, and had them privately printed in a *Documentary Life of Nathan Hale*. In the selections below we can read at first hand, in the words of both his friends and his foes, a story that has inspirited generations of Hale's countrymen.

Following his graduation from Yale in 1773 at the age of eighteen, Hale taught school for a time in his native Connecticut. Then, on July 1, 1775—two months

In the British artillery park, probably located near 66th Street and Third Avenue, New York, brave young Captain Hale faces his executioners. This anonymous painting of 1820 erroneously shows the hero's hair in a queue.

after Lexington and Concord—he was commissioned a lieutenant in the Continental Army, and closed his one-room school in New London, a building still proudly preserved by the town. We see him first in the reminiscences of a comrade-in-arms, Lieutenant Elisha Bostwick:

. . . I can now in imagination see his person & hear his voice—his person I should say was a little above the common stature in height, his shoulders of a moderate breadth, his limbs strait & very plump: regular features—very fair skin—blue eyes—flaxen or very light hair which was always kept short—his eyebrows a shade darker than his hair & his voice rather sharp or piercing—his bodily agility was remarkable. I have seen him follow a football & kick it over the tops of the trees in the Bowery at New York, (an exercise which he was fond of)—his mental powers seemed to be above the common sort—his mind of a sedate and sober cast, & he was undoubtedly Pious; for it was remark'd that when any of the soldiers of his company were sick he always visited them & usually Prayed for & with them in their sickness. . . .

Early in the fall of 1776, after being disastrously defeated on Long Island, Washington needed to know the dispositions and the intentions of the British forces. Hale and other officers of the picked regiment known as Knowlton's Rangers were asked to volunteer for an intelligence mission behind enemy lines. On the first call, none responded; on the second, Nathan Hale alone stepped forward. A little later he told his friend Captain (afterward General) William Hull what he had done:

[Hale] asked my candid opinion [says Hull's memoir]. I replied, that it was an action which involved serious consequences, and the propriety of it was doubtful . . . Stratagems are resorted to in war; they are feints and evasions, performed under no disguise . . . and, considered in a military view, lawful and advantageous. . . . But who respects the character of a spy, assuming the garb of friendship but to betray? . . . I ended by saying, that should he undertake the enterprise, his short, bright career, would close with an ignominious death.

He replied, "I am fully sensible of the consequences of discovery and capture in such a situation. . . . Yet . . . I wish to be useful, and every kind of service, necessary to the public good, becomes honourable by being necessary. If the exigencies of my country demand a peculiar service, its claims to perform that service are imperious."

Sergeant Stephen Hempstead of New London accompanied him as he set out on his mission from Norwalk, Connecticut:

Capt. Hale had a general order to all armed vessels, to take him to any place he should designate: he was set across the Sound . . . at Huntington (Long-Island) . . . Capt. Hale had changed his uniform for a plain suit of citizens brown clothes, with a round broad-brimmed hat, assuming the character of a Dutch school-master, leaving all his other clothes, commission, public and private papers, with me, and also his silver shoe buckles, saying they would not comport with his character of school-master, and retaining nothing but his College diploma, as an introduction to his assumed calling. Thus equipped, we parted . . .

Hale's servant, Asher Wright, who had remained behind, told what happened next:

He passed all their guards on Long Island, went over to New York in a ferryboat & got by all the guards but the last.

They stopped him, searched & found drawings of the works, with descriptions in Latin, under the inner sole of the pumps which he wore. Some say his cousin, Samuel Hale, a tory, betrayed him. I don't know; guess he did.

"Betrayed" is probably too strong; "identified" is closer to the truth. A surviving letter from Samuel, a Harvard man (1766), seems to deny any misdeed, or at least any guilt, as the story was spread in a Newburyport newspaper—but he thereafter fled to England and never returned to America, even after the war, for his wife and son.

The next day a kind-hearted British officer, Captain John Montresor, approached the American lines under a flag of truce to report the inevitable denouement. Captain Hull recorded Montresor's words:

. . . Hale at once declared his name, his rank in the American army, and his object in coming within the British lines.

Sir William Howe, without the form of a trial, gave orders for his execution the following morning. He was placed in the custody of the Provost Marshal, who was . . . hardened to human suffering and every softening sentiment of the heart. Captain Hale, alone, without sympathy or support, save that from above, on the near approach of death asked for a clergyman to attend him. It was refused. He then requested a Bible; that too was refused by his inhuman jailer.

On the morning of his execution . . . my station was near the fatal spot, and I requested the Provost Marshal to permit the prisoner to sit in my marquee, while he was making the necessary preparations. Captain Hale entered: he was calm, and bore himself with gentle dignity, in the consciousness of rectitude and high intentions. He asked for writing materials, which I furnished him: he wrote two letters . . . He was shortly after summoned to the gallows. But a few persons were around him, yet his characteristic dying words were remembered. He said, "I only regret, that I have but one life to lose for my country."

A brief excerpt from a letter written at Coventry, Connecticut, the following spring by Nathan Hale's father, Richard, who had six sons altogether in the Revolution, betrays the deep grief of this unlettered man:

. . . you desired me to inform you about my son Nathan . . . he was executed about the 22nd of September Last by the Aconts we have had. A Child I sot much by but he is gone . . .

This letter, addressed to Richard Hale's brother, Major Samuel Hale, in Portsmouth, New Hampshire, on March 28, 1777, was put away in a secret drawer of the Major's desk. In 1908, the old desk was sold at auction as an antique, and three years later the new owner, the Honorable Frank L. Howe of Barrington, New Hampshire, chanced upon it. Such is the thrill of historical discovery.

PLESSY v. FERGUSON

The Birth

In the spring of 1885, Charles Dudley Warner, Mark Twain's friend, neighbor, and onetime collaborator from Hartford, Connecticut, visited the International Exposition at New Orleans. He was astonished to find that "white and colored people mingled freely, talking and looking at what was of common interest," that Negroes "took their full share of the parade and the honors," and that the two races associated "in unconscious equality of privileges." During his visit he saw "a colored clergyman in his surplice seated in the chancel of the most important white Episcopal church in New Orleans, assisting in the service."

It was a common occurrence in the 1880's for foreign travellers and northern visitors to comment, sometimes with distaste and always with surprise, on the freedom of association between white and colored people in the South. Yankees in particular were unprepared for what they found and sometimes estimated that conditions below the Potomac were better than those above. There was discrimination, to be sure, and Negroes were often excluded from first-class public accommodations—as they were in the North. But that was done on the responsibility of private owners or managers and not by requirement of law. According to the Supreme Court's decision in the Civil Rights Cases of 1883 the federal law gave no protection from such private acts.

Where discrimination existed it was often erratic and inconsistent. On trains the usual practice was to exclude Negroes from first-class or "ladies'" cars but to permit them to mix with whites in second-class or "smoking" cars. In the old seaboard states of the South, however, Negroes were as free to ride first class as whites. In no state was segregation on trains complete, and in none was it enforced by law. The age of Jim Crow was still to come.

The first genuine Jim Crow law requiring railroads to carry Negroes in separate cars or behind partitions was adopted by Florida in 1887. Mississippi followed this example in 1888; Texas in 1889; Louisiana in 1890; Alabama, Arkansas, Georgia, and Tennessee in 1891; and Kentucky in 1892. The Carolinas and Virginia did not fall into line until the last three years of the century.

Negroes watched with despair while the legal foundations for the Jim Crow system were laid and the walls of segregation mounted around them. Their disenchantment with the hopes based on the Civil War amendments and the Reconstruction laws was nearly complete by 1890. The American commitment to equality, solemnly attested by three amendments to the Constitution and by elaborate civil rights acts, was virtually repudiated. The "compromise of 1877" between the Hayes Republicans and the southern conservatives had resulted in the withdrawal of federal troops from the South and the formal end of Reconstruction. What had started then as a retreat had within a decade turned into a rout. Northern radicals and liberals had abandoned the cause; the courts had rendered the Constitution helpless; the Republican party had forsaken the cause it had sponsored. A tide of racism was mounting in the country unopposed.

The colored community of New Orleans, with its strong infusion of French and other nationalities, was in a strategic position to furnish leadership for the resistance against segregation. Many of these people had culture, education, and some wealth, as well as a heri-

of Jim Crow

By C. VANN WOODWARD

tage of several generations of freedom. Unlike the great majority of Negroes, they were city people with an established professional class and a high degree of literacy. By ancestry as well as by residence they were associated with Latin cultures at variance with Anglo-American ideas of race relations. Their forebears had lived under the Code Noir decreed for Louisiana by Louis XIV, and their city faced out upon Latin America.

When the Jim Crow car bill was introduced in the Louisiana legislature, New Orleans Negroes organized to fight it. Negroes were still voting in large numbers, and there were sixteen colored senators and representatives in the Louisiana General Assembly. On May 24, 1890, that body received "A Protest of the American Citizens' Equal Rights Association of Louisiana Against Class Legislation." An organization of colored people, the association protested that the pending bill was "unconstitutional, unamerican, unjust, dangerous and against sound public policy." It would, declared the protest, "be a free license to the evilly-disposed that they might with impunity insult, humiliate, and other-

wise maltreat inoffensive persons, and especially women and children who should happen to have a dark skin."

On July 10, 1890, the Assembly passed the bill, the governor signed it, and it became law. Entitled "An Act to promote the comfort of passengers," the new law required railroads "to provide equal but separate accommodations for the white and colored races." Two members of the Equal Rights Association, L. A. Martinet, editor of the New Orleans *Crusader,* and R. L. Desdunes, placed heavy blame on the sixteen colored members of the Assembly for the passage of the bill. According to Martinet, "they were completely the masters of the situation." They had but to withhold their support for a bill desired by the powerful Louisiana Lottery Company until the Jim Crow bill was killed. "But in an evil moment," he added, "our Representatives turned their ears to listen to the golden siren," and "did so for a 'consideration.'"

Putting aside recriminations, the *Crusader* declared: "The Bill is now a law. The next thing is what we are going to do?" The editor spoke testily of boycotting the railroads, but concluded that "the next

Albion W. Tourgée   *Justice John M. Harlan*

"Jim Crow" as a social reality began much later, with separate-car laws like that tested before the Supreme Court in 1896. Albion Tourgée's arguments in behalf of Homer Plessy, a Louisiana Negro, moved only Justice Harlan; the majority decision, read by Justice Brown, became the legal basis for complete segregation of the races.

Justice Henry B. Brown

thing is . . . to begin to gather funds to test the constitutionality of this law. We'll make a case, a test case, and bring it before the Federal Courts." On September 1, 1891, a group of eighteen men of color formed a "Citizens' Committee to Test the Constitutionality of the Separate Car Law."

Money came in slowly at first, but by October 11, Martinet could write that the committee had already collected $1,500 and that more could be expected "after we have the case well started." Even before the money was collected, Martinet had opened a correspondence about the case with Albion Winegar Tourgée of Mayville, New York, and on October 10 the Citizens' Committee formally elected Tourgée "leading counsel in the case, from beginning to end, with power to choose associates."

This action called back into the stream of history a name prominent in the annals of Reconstruction. Albion Tourgée was in 1890 probably the most famous surviving carpetbagger. His fame was due not so much to his achievements as a carpetbagger in North Caro-

After Plessy v. Ferguson, *Negro allegiance was divided. The conservative majority followed Booker T. Washington (seen above in 1901), who in his "Atlanta Compromise" speech of 1895 had told his fellow Negroes that the fulfillment of their goals lay in self-improvement, and that "agitation of questions of social equality is the extremest folly . . ."*

lina, significant though they were, as to the six novels about his Reconstruction experiences that he had published since 1879. Born in Ohio, of French Huguenot descent, he had served as an officer in the Union Army, and moved to Greensboro, North Carolina, in 1865 to practice law. He soon became a leader of the Radical Republican party, took a prominent part in writing the Radical Constitution of North Carolina, and served as a judge of the superior court for six years with considerable distinction. He brought to the fight against segregation in Louisiana a combination of zeal and ability that the Citizens' Committee of New Orleans would have found it hard to duplicate. They had reason to write him, "we know we have a friend in you & we know your ability is beyond question." He was informed that the committee's decision was made "spontaneously, warmly, & gratefully."

Tourgée's first suggestion was that the person chosen for defendant in the test case be "nearly white," but that proposal raised some doubts. "It would be quite difficult," explained Martinet, "to have a lady *too* nearly white refused admission to a 'white' car." He pointed out that "people of tolerably fair complexion, even if unmistakably colored, enjoy here a large degree of immunity from the accursed prejudice. . . . To make this case would require some tact." He would volunteer himself, "but I am one of those whom a fair complexion favors. I go everywhere, in all public places, though well-known all over the city, & never is anything said to me. On the cars it would be the same thing. In fact, color prejudice, in this respect does not affect me. But, as I have said, we can try it, with another."

Railroad officials proved surprisingly co-operative. The first one approached, however, confessed that his road "did not enforce the law." It provided the Jim Crow car and posted the required sign, but told its conductors to molest no one who ignored instructions. Officers of two other roads "said the law was a bad and mean one; they would like to get rid of it," and asked for time to consult counsel. "They want to help us," said Martinet, "but dread public opinion." The extra expense of separate cars was one reason for railroad opposition to the Jim Crow law.

It was finally agreed that a white passenger should object to the presence of a Negro in a "white" coach, that the conductor should direct the colored passenger to go to the Jim Crow car, and that he should refuse to go. "The conductor will be instructed not to use force or molest," reported Martinet, "& our white passenger will swear out the affidavit. This will give us our *habeas corpus* case, I hope." On the appointed day, February 24, 1892, Daniel F. Desdunes, a young colored man, bought a ticket for Mobile, boarded the

Louisville & Nashville Railroad, and took a seat in the white coach.

All went according to plan. Desdunes was committed for trial to the Criminal District Court in New Orleans and released on bail. On March 21, James C. Walker, a local attorney associated with Tourgée in the case, filed a plea protesting that his client was not guilty and attacking the constitutionality of the Jim Crow law. He wrote Tourgée that he intended to go to trial as early as he could.

Between the lawyers there was not entire agreement on procedure. Walker favored the plea that the law was void because it attempted to regulate interstate commerce, over which the Supreme Court held that Congress had exclusive jurisdiction. Tourgée was doubtful. "What we want," he wrote Walker, "is not a verdict of not guilty, nor a defect in this law but a decision whether such a law can be legally enacted and enforced in any state and we should get everything off the track and out of the way for such a decision." Walker confessed that "it's hard for me to give up my pet hobby that the law is void as a regulation of interstate commerce," and Tourgée admitted that he "may have spoken too lightly of the interstate commerce matter."

The discussion was ended abruptly and the whole approach altered before Desdunes' case came to trial by a decision of the Louisiana Supreme Court handed down on May 25. In this case, which was of entirely independent origin, the court reversed the ruling of a lower court and upheld the Pullman Company's plea that the Jim Crow law was unconstitutional in so far as it applied to interstate passengers.

Desdunes was an interstate passenger holding a ticket to Alabama, but the decision was a rather empty victory. The law still applied to intrastate passengers, and since all states adjacent to Louisiana had by this time adopted similar or identical Jim Crow laws, the exemption of interstate passengers was of no great importance to the Negroes of Louisiana, and it left the principle against which they contended unchallenged. On June 1, Martinet wired Tourgée on behalf of the committee, saying that "Walker wants new case wholly within state limits," and asking Tourgée's opinion. Tourgée wired his agreement.

One week later, on June 7, Homer Adolph Plessy bought a ticket in New Orleans, boarded the East Louisiana Railroad bound for Covington, a destination "wholly within the state limits," and took a seat in the white coach. Since Plessy later described himself as "seven-eighths Caucasian and one-eighth African blood," and swore that "the admixture of colored blood is not discernible," it may be assumed that the railroad had been told of the plan and had agreed to

co-operate. When Plessy refused to comply with the conductor's request that he move to the Jim Crow car, he was arrested by Detective Christopher C. Cain "and quietly accompanied the officer." The New Orleans *Times-Democrat* remarked that "It is generally believed that Plessy intends testing the law before the courts."

In due course Homer Plessy's case became *Plessy v. Ferguson*. The latter name belonged to John H. Ferguson, Judge of Section A of the Criminal District Court for the Parish of New Orleans, who overruled the plea of Tourgée and Walker, the defendant's counsel, that the Jim Crow law was null and void because it was in conflict with the Constitution of the United States. Plessy then applied to the State Supreme Court for a writ of prohibition and certiorari and was given a hearing in November, 1892. The court recognized that neither the interstate commerce clause nor the question of equality of accommodations was involved and held that "the sole question" was whether a law requiring "separate but equal accommodations" violated

CONTINUED ON PAGE 100

FROM *A Pictorial History of the Negro in America* BY LANGSTON HUGHES AND MILTON MELTZER

More militant Negroes, led by the late W. E. B. Du Bois (second from the right in the second row), met near Niagara Falls in 1905 to form the Niagara Movement, forerunner of the N.A.A.C.P. Backing Washington's plea for Negro education but not his civil-rights stand, the Movement's leaders said: "We want full manhood suffrage, and we want it now."

A Pennsylvania Dutch harvest festival, pictured in 1853 by an unknown artist, radiates Gemütlichkeit. *While a few participants are slicin*

"Fill yourself up, clea

…d boiling apples—to make apple mead, a kind of wine—most are simply enjoying the music and generous samples of last year's product.

"...our plate"

Among the Pennsylvania Dutch, both plain and fancy, the milk is yet, the *schnitz-un-gnepp* delights the soul, and the soup is thick enough to stand on

By ARCHIE ROBERTSON

At the close of the nineteenth century Rudyard Kipling saw southeastern Pennsylvania as a land of "little houses and bursting big barns, fat cattle, fat women, and all as peaceful as Heaven might be if they farmed there." This is the home of the Pennsylvania Dutch, and even today, when the face of rural America elsewhere has changed drastically in appearance, the Pennsylvania Dutch region still looks much the same.

It is a country of "fatness," in the fine, Old Testament phrase. Its well-watered farms, fertilized and guarded against soil erosion for centuries, have improved with the passage of time until they have become the most valuable nonirrigated farmland in the United States. From the same rich soil the towns and cities of mellow red-brick houses draw their own character. At the food stalls in the farmers' markets of Lancaster, Mennonite and Amish ladies in trim bonnets preside over the most appetizing array of food to be found anywhere—fresh butter elegantly stamped by a mold which is a family treasure, bursting white cauliflowers, mountains of golden pumpkins, and stacks of gay cakes and cookies, shoo-fly pies, smoked hams, and sausages. A glorious army of glass jars contains the homemade condiments—including pickled oysters, corn relish, fox-grape jelly, apple butter, and ginger pears—from which a Pennsylvania housewife selects the "seven sweets and seven sours" which traditionally accompany a meal.

Here, over a period of nearly three hundred years, has grown up the most enduring American regional cuisine. Well into the age of advanced homogenization, Pennsylvania Dutch cooking has held its own. It has done even better. As billboards along the highways attest, it has become a major tourist attraction. From all over America, as they have been doing for a long time, people come here just to eat.

It is interesting to speculate why. The Pennsylvania Dutch are predominantly German in origin—with a strong admixture of Swiss, Moravians, and some Hollanders among them—and many of their favorite dishes, like sauerkraut and pickled pig's feet, are available anywhere that Germans have foregathered. Others which the Pennsylvania Dutch can take credit for introducing, like scrapple, waffles, apple butter, and Philadelphia pepper pot, have long since joined the nationwide menu. Still others, of course, like chicken corn soup or *schnitz-un-gnepp* (made with slices of dried apple soaked back to original size, dumplings, and ham or pork), are available only here. No one else seems to know how to make a shoo-fly pie from molasses, brown sugar, flour, and spices. (The name may

have come from the fact that a cook working with these ingredients on a hot summer day would have winged visitors.) But the genius of this cuisine lies not so much in its unique dishes as in the fresh touch which these people give to the conventional American food obtainable anywhere. They have quite a way with common things.

They are gifted pancake cooks, for instance. Their buckwheat cakes may contain—besides buckwheat flour—corn meal, potato water, and a touch of molasses. The Pennsylvania Dutch know how to bring to greatness a simple meal like the classic breakfast of fried mush, fried apples, and sausages. They are connoisseurs of corn-meal mush, to begin with, always choosing yellow meal, preferably from corn that has been roasted for extra flavor before grinding. And unlike New Englanders with their "hasty pudding," the Pennsylvania Dutch like to let mush bubble happily away in a big iron pot for hours. They may eat it hot with cold milk or cold with hot milk, but always with a puddle of melted butter in the middle. When it is fried, they pour all sorts of good things over it—old-fashioned dark molasses from a country store, comb honey, pure maple syrup, or their own apple butter, which is dark and spicy with cloves, cinnamon, or sassafras and quite different from that found elsewhere.

They choose the tastiest kind of apples for frying, depending on the season, for they have a choice of many kinds on the orchard slopes of their misty blue hills. The apples, of course, are lightly sprinkled with powdered sugar and cinnamon before serving. The sausage is homemade, delicately seasoned and smoked.

This is a cuisine of abundance, created by thrift and hard work. "Fill yourself up, clean your plate," is a popular motto.

Like the people themselves, their cooking can be either plain or fancy—parsnip fritters or oysters and caviar. Both varieties will be good, and both, whatever the more exquisite type of gourmet may think, could well appear on the same table. This cuisine is completely without class consciousness. What is good—and not what is novel, fashionable, or easy to fix—determines what the Pennsylvania Dutch eat and serve to their guests. "No trouble," they always say politely to appreciative visitors. By this, they do not really mean that good cooking is no trouble. They mean simply that the results are worth it, in terms of human happiness.

Appetite is the basis of any good cuisine, but the roots of Pennsylvania Dutch cuisine go even deeper than this, into a background of suffering and privation which drove them from the Old World to the New. Here they created on free soil an authentic, distinct culture of which their food is only one—although a

Lewis Miller, an artistically inclined carpenter of York, Pa., kept a pictorial diary of nineteenth-century Pennsylvania life—nearly 2,000 colored drawings. Right, a busy cook wields a wooden spatula, used to get baked goods in and out of the big brick ovens.

Miller sketched a pleasant scene at a local brewery: a congeries of housewives and children come to purchase some yeast. The artist's perspective was undeniably peculiar; but his subject, here as usual, was representative of the rural life he knew so well.

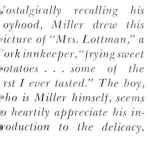

Nostalgically recalling his boyhood, Miller drew this picture of "Mrs. Lottman," a York innkeeper, "frying sweet potatoes . . . some of the first I ever tasted." The boy, who is Miller himself, seems to heartily appreciate his introduction to the delicacy.

very important—element. This particular regional cookery is like living history. So, in some ways, are the people themselves—especially the Plain People.

Outstanding among these are the Amish, who still wear black hats and long beards, drive their buggies along Lancaster County roads, and fasten their outer clothes with hooks instead of with buttons, which were associated with the nobility and the military. Their ancestors first began to come to southeastern Pennsylvania in the seventeenth century. Conditions in the Palatinate—a province of the Rhineland in Germany—had been nothing less than dreadful. Beginning with the Thirty Years' War in 1618, there were persecutions of Protestants by Catholics, of Catholics by Protestants, and—most bitterly sometimes—of Protestants by Protestants. Toward the end of the century, an especially vindictive army from France invaded the Palatinate and took pains to cut down the fruit trees, dig up the vineyards, burn the farmhouses, and turn the people out in the dead of winter. Their sufferings were observed with sympathy by William Penn, who was planning a commonwealth in the New World devoted to religious liberty—and peace. He circulated his prospectus throughout the Rhineland and twice visited the region in person to invite its distressed survivors to join him. The Mennonites—followers of Menno Simons, an early sixteenth-century religious reformer—were the first to accept. In 1683, at Germantown, near Philadelphia, they made the first German settlement in America.

The Mennonites were Plain People, members of the

radical wing of the Reformation which disavowed all established churches, Protestant as well as Catholic, sought to recover the simplicity of New Testament Christianity, practiced pacifism, and, to emphasize their separateness from the world, dressed in plain, dark clothes. They were, of course, pleased that their new Quaker neighbors also "dressed plain," were pacifists, and held religious views not unlike their own. Other Mennonites soon came, and other Plain People of various kinds—the Dunkards, or Brethren, who baptized by total immersion three times; Moravians from Bohemia, followers of John Huss, who was burned at the stake in 1415; and a small group called Schwenkfelders, who like the Moravians had been persecuted for centuries, driven from one country to another across the map of Europe.

They all arrived hungry, if only from the long sea voyage. The Schwenkfelders, when their ship dropped anchor in 1734 near New Castle, Delaware, obtained their first fresh water in months, along with apples and fresh bread. They still commemorate this occasion each September, sharing, after church service, a meal of the same basic ingredients—apple butter, fresh bread, butter, and water, "spiced," as a Quaker observer noted, "with cheerful talk."

In one way or another food became a sort of religious symbol with all of the Plain People. After worship, the Dunkards held love feasts, suppers at which the main dish was a lamb stew commemorating the paschal lamb. The House Amish, fundamentalist Mennonites who felt their brethren were backsliding, held their services in each other's homes and followed them with a memorable dinner for all. The Moravians, at Bethlehem, became famous for their baking. Their delicate

TEXT CONTINUED ON PAGE 64

Utensils of good living: Plain enough in function, old Pennsylvania Dutch gastronomic equipment was fancy in decoration. The ceramic dish above, inscribed to one Cadarina Raeder, is typical in colors and motifs. At far left (opposite page) is a graceful toleware teapot; then a waffle iron, an earthenware jug, a tray, and (below) a pie crimper.

PHOTO, VINCENT TORTORA

A tenacious way of life: This recent photograph of a group of Amish children outside their one-room school-house in Stumptown, Lancaster County, Pa., suggests one reason for the steadfast quality of Pennsylvania Dutch cuisine. The Amish habitually look with vast suspicion upon anything newfangled—in education or whatever— but they cling to those things they have found good, including the traditional dishes and recipes of their sect.

love feasts consisted of rolls and a beverage, served in church and shared in a spirit of devotion and brotherhood.

The Plain People were followed to America in the early eighteenth century by many of the "church people," members of the Reformed and Lutheran churches, with some Catholics, too, who had remained behind in the Rhineland. (These, of course, were the "gay" or "fancy" Dutch, and their descendants in southeastern Pennsylvania came to outnumber the "plain" Dutch by ten to one.)

Conditions in the Palatinate had not much improved. In the terrible winter of 1709, it was so cold that birds allegedly froze in the air, and wild beasts, in the forest. Men looked into each other's eyes, one historian reported, and said, "Let us go to America; and if we perish, we perish." Pennsylvania, however, was not their original destination. Queen Anne of England invited the Lutherans and Reformed to go to New York, which the English had taken over from Holland.

 his frightfully mismanaged project provided the gay Dutch with a legend of suffering almost equal to anything the Plain People had known. On shipboard, with inadequate food and no sanitation and no light or air below decks, they died by the hundreds. By the time they reached New York Harbor, typhus had broken out. They were installed in tents on Governors Island, where hundreds more died of disease and as the result of the rigors of the voyage. The survivors were sent up the Hudson, told to build their own villages, and fed salty meat and short rations of bread. A minister among them wrote home that "they boil grass and ye children eat the leaves of the trees." When a letter of invitation reached them from Pennsylvania, one hardy band accepted. After that the church people emigrated from the Rhineland direct to Pennsylvania.

Now the plain and the fancy, reunited on the rich soil in the valleys of the Susquehanna, the Lehigh, and the Schuylkill north of Philadelphia, began to build the culture that became known as Pennsylvania Dutch, because to their eighteenth-century neighbors anyone speaking any variant of the German language was a Dutchman (Deutscher). And it was in fact their particular dialect which did most to unite them and keep them separate from other Americans. That dialect, which can still be understood in parts of the Rhineland today, is neither the "Low Dutch" of Holland nor the "High Dutch," or classical German, in which their Bibles were printed. Thus, it distinguished them both from other German immigrants who came later and

from their "Low Dutch" neighbors in New York, as well as from the English-speaking Quakers, Episcopalians, and Presbyterians all around them. It was a language without a written literature, and for centuries they lived in a world apart, continuing to paint hex signs on their barns and observing many other Old World customs which had long ago died out elsewhere. Several of their own words, of course—like "dunking," for a local custom with doughnuts which became widespread—joined the American language.

In a strange, wonderful way Pennsylvania Dutch—as Englished—makes very good sense. "My off is on," for instance, means "My vacation has started." "Do you think it will make down?" is "Will it rain?" Or, "the cream is all,"—gone, of course—"the milk is yet." And there is the classic story of a sign on a front door, "Bell don't make—Bump." But all these are the trivial aspects of this culture. Its mainspring, which set it going, was the common memory of the fertile, lovingly cared-for farms and orchards of the Rhineland, and as rapidly as they could clear the forests the Pennsylvania Dutch set out to reproduce these in Pennsylvania and to stock their larders.

In anything pertaining to food they were especially inventive. To bring home more game, they designed a longer, more accurate rifle, mistakenly called the Kentucky rifle after Daniel Boone took it there from Pennsylvania. The first American cookstove was cast here, at Mary Ann Furnace in 1765. They made a long-handled waffle iron, imprinting a tulip design, for use on the open hearth. Instead of diamonds, which were notably scarce, young men gave their sweethearts handsomely carved rolling pins as engagement presents.

In fact, a rich folk art grew up around their cooking and eating. Many of their early stoves were so decorated with biblical scenes that they have been called "the Bible in iron." Henry William Stiegel's glassware, a treasure today, was blown here, and they made gay pottery. And inevitably, from this rich soil and these busy kitchens a surplus of food began to emerge. Therefore the Pennsylvania Dutch invented the great Conestoga wagon, a ship on wheels, to transport their produce to fairs and farmers' markets. Since good food knows no language barrier, their own diet became the standard for the region. For example, the bachelor President James Buchanan, a Lancaster man, was famous for his sauerkraut suppers after he left office; he won the hearts of a Dutch family with whom he sheltered one night by insisting that the big bowl of corn-meal mush which was all they had planned for supper was exactly what he wanted.

By the time of the American Revolution, Philadelphia had become famous as the capital of a land of good eating, and one of its Pennsylvania Dutch bakers

CONTINUED ON PAGE 80

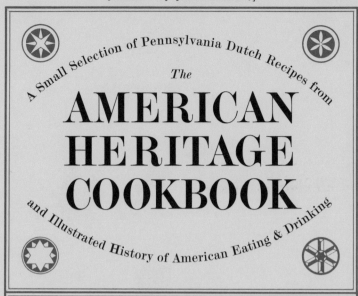

A Small Selection of Pennsylvania Dutch Recipes from

The

AMERICAN HERITAGE COOKBOOK

and Illustrated History of American Eating & Drinking

SCRAPPLE

1½ pounds pork shoulder
¼ pound pork liver
1 cup yellow corn meal
2 teaspoons salt
¼ cup finely chopped onions

Dash of ground cloves
¼ teaspoon dried thyme
1 teaspoon dried sage
1 teaspoon dried marjoram
½ teaspoon ground pepper

Combine pork shoulder and liver in a saucepan with one quart of water and cook over moderate heat for one hour. Drain, reserving the broth. Discard all bones and chop the meat fine. Blend corn meal, salt, one cup of water, and two cups of the broth in a saucepan. Cook, stirring constantly, until thick. Stir in meat, onions, spices, and herbs. Cover and simmer gently for about an hour over a very low heat. Pour into a 9″ x 5″ x 3″ loaf pan and chill until firm. Cut into slices about one half to three quarters of an inch thick, dust lightly with flour, and fry in a little heated shortening over moderate heat until crisp on both sides. Serve at once.

APPLE BUTTER

3 quarts sweet cider
8 pounds ripe, well-flavored apples
2½ cups brown sugar, firmly packed

2 teaspoons cloves
2 teaspoons cinnamon
1 teaspoon allspice
½ teaspoon salt

Cook cider over a high heat (without a cover) until it is reduced to half, about 30 minutes. Add washed, cored, and quartered unpeeled apples and cook over a low heat until very tender. Stir frequently. Work apple mixture through a sieve, returning the purée to the kettle. Stir in sugar, spices, and salt. Cook over very low heat, stirring almost continuously, until apple butter thickens. Pour into four sterilized pint jars and seal securely.

TO OUR READERS:

REGULAR EDITION

Here is the book from which the preceding article and the recipes on the nondetachable part of this page are taken. It will be published in August. It is an entertaining and authoritative two-part volume of history and cookery. Part I describes in detail the story behind America's remarkably varied foods and eating and drinking habits. Part II contains more than 500 recipes for dishes and drinks that originated here or were brought to this country from many lands.

The Regular Edition is one 640-page, 6⅜″ by 9¼″ volume. The De Luxe Edition is published in two handsomely bound volumes—history in one, recipes in the other—and comes in a heavy protective slipcase.

On the reverse side you will find more information about the scope and plan of this unique approach to American history, and a list of the authors and experts who contributed to it. To reserve an advance copy (it will be shipped in early summer) at the 28 per cent discount offered to subscribers of AMERICAN HERITAGE, fill in, detach, and mail the coupon below.

DE LUXE EDITION

AMERICAN HERITAGE BOOK SERVICE OFFICES
334 West Center St., Marion, Ohio   43301

Please send me a copy of THE AMERICAN HERITAGE COOKBOOK *and Illustrated History of American Eating & Drinking* when it comes off the press in June. I may return the book within two weeks if it is not what I want, and pay nothing. If I keep it, I will pay for the edition checked.

☐ REGULAR—pre-publication price, $8.95 (plus postage and packing), instead of the $12.50 retail price.

☐ DE LUXE—add $2.50.

These terms are offered to AMERICAN HERITAGE subscribers who reserve before publication date.

NAME_____
(please print)

STREET_____

CITY_____ZONE_____

STATE_____

X9073

THE AMERICAN HERITAGE COOKBOOK
and Illustrated History of American Eating & Drinking

SIZE: 640 pages; 6⅜″ by 9¼″.

ILLUSTRATIONS: More than 350, 95 in color, including period paintings, drawings, prints, photographs.

SCOPE: From the days of the early settlers to the turn of the twentieth century.

PLAN: Nine essays that explore the historical factors in the development of American eating and drinking; nine profiles of men and women who helped to mould, or in some way reflect, our changing tastes in food and drink; nine picture sections highlighting the period and the person, plus more than 500 tested recipes and 30 historical menus.

AUTHORS: Cleveland Amory, Lucius Beebe, Gerald Carson, Paul Engle, Marshall Fishwick, Evan Jones, Leonard Levinson, Russell Lynes, Archie Robertson, George Willison.

EXPERTS: Helen Duprey Bullock, Food Historian; Helen McCully Associates, Food Consultants.

SCHNITZ-UN-GNEPP

| 2½ to 3 pounds smoked ham with bone | 2 tablespoons brown sugar |
| 2 cups dried apples | Dumplings |

Cover ham almost completely with cold water. Bring to a boil, reduce heat, cover and simmer gently for about two hours. While the ham is simmering, put the dried apples (*Schnitz*) in a bowl, cover with cold water, and soak. When the ham has cooked, add drained apples and brown sugar. Simmer for another hour. Serve with dumplings, made as follows:

1½ cups all-purpose flour	1 tablespoon butter
3 teaspoons baking powder	¼ cup milk, approximately
½ teaspoon salt	1 egg, well beaten

Sift flour, baking powder, and salt together into a bowl. Pinch in the butter until well distributed, then stir in enough milk to make a soft dough, and add egg. Lift the cooked ham onto a hot platter and spoon apples around it. Drop dumplings (*Gnepp*) from a spoon into the boiling ham liquid, cover tightly, and simmer 10 to 12 minutes. Arrange the dumplings on the platter around the meat, and spoon a little of the liquid over them. Some Pennsylvania Dutch cooks thicken the liquid by stirring in a little flour mixed to a smooth paste with water; others like it unthickened. Serves 6 to 8.

SHOO-FLY PIE

Pastry for a one-crust pie

CRUMB MIXTURE:	FILLING:
1½ cups all-purpose flour	½ teaspoon baking soda
½ cup brown sugar, firmly packed	½ cup molasses
Pinch of salt	½ cup boiling water
1 big pinch each of ginger and nutmeg	⅔ of crumb mixture
½ teaspoon cinnamon	
¼ cup soft butter	

Line an eight-inch pie pan with pastry. Refrigerate while you prepare the crumb mixture and filling. Combine flour with brown sugar, salt, and spices. Work or pinch in the butter until mealy. Stir baking soda, molasses, and boiling water together. Stir in two thirds of the crumb mixture and pour into the unbaked pie shell. Sprinkle top with remaining third of the crumbs and bake in a preheated oven at 375 degrees for 30 to 40 minutes, or until crust and crumbs are golden brown. Cool before serving.

THE CITY *of the* LIVING GOD

From a long-obscure life of Cortés, written by his own secretary, comes a narrative of the incredible splendors of Moctezuma's Aztec capital

By FRANCISCO LÓPEZ DE GÓMARA   *Translated by* LESLEY BYRD SIMPSON

To that small group of Spaniards who early in November, 1519, first glimpsed the city of Mexico (or Tenochtitlán, as the Indians also called it), the sight must have been unforgettable. "It is like the enchantments they tell of in the legend of Amadis!" one exclaimed. "Are not the things we see a dream?" Here was no scattering of primitive native huts but a magnificent city of stone rising from an island in a lake. It was as if the newcomers had suddenly found themselves transported to the Age of the Pharaohs—for such was the level which the Aztec Indian culture had attained. Indeed, the city of Moctezuma, a man revered as a god by his own people, matched in splendor anything Europe could offer. Today it seems incredible that a force of perhaps four hundred men could overthrow a civilization so advanced and so apparently powerful. But numbers in this case are meaningless, for Moctezuma and his wide-ranging Aztec empire had encountered one of the most daring and resourceful captains of history, Hernán Cortés. He was a man whom the Indians regarded as a god in his own right—until, too late, they discovered that his motives were all too human. The following account is taken from the classic but little-known life of Cortés written by Francisco López de Gómara in 1552. Gómara was eminently qualified for the task, for he served as Cortés' chaplain and secretary from 1541 until the conquistador's death in 1547. Surprisingly, though the book has long been a source for historians, it has had but one English translation—and that a much-mutilated version which appeared in 1578. This modern edition is the work of Lesley Byrd Simpson, Professor Emeritus of Spanish at the University of California; under the title *Cortés: The Life of the Conqueror by His Secretary*, it will soon be published by the University of California Press.

AMERICAN MUSEUM OF NATURAL HISTORY

Legend says a magical mirror embedded in the head of a bird warned Moctezuma of the Spanish conquest.

Mounted on the horses that the Indians regarded as supernatural creatures, Cortés and his men are met by Aztec warriors on the causeway leading to the city of Mexico. The pictures reproduced here are, with one exception, taken from an illustrated manuscript of the mid-sixteenth century, the Codex Florentino. It was prepared by Indians under the supervision of Fray Bernardino de Sahagún, who, a generation after the conquest, attempted to depict the culture and history of a civilization that was already little more than a memory.

IXTAPALAPA IS CONNECTED WITH MEXICO by two leagues of a very wide causeway, wide enough to accommodate eight horses abreast, and as straight as if drawn with a ruler. The gates of Mexico could be discerned by one with good eyesight. Along its length are Mexicalcingo, of about 4,000 houses, all built over the water; Coyoacán, of 6,000; and Churubusco, of 5,000. These cities are adorned with many temples, each with its tower. . . .

Cortés, with his 400 companions and 6,000 Indian friends from the pacified towns, advanced along this causeway, marching with great difficulty because of the pressure of the crowds that came out to see them. As he drew near to the city he came to the junction of another causeway which was protected by a large stone bastion, two fathoms high, with towers at the two ends, between them a crenelated gallery and two gates, very strong. Here some 4,000 gentlemen of the court were waiting to receive him, richly dressed after their fashion, all in the same style. Upon his approach each of them touched the earth with his right hand, kissed it, bowed, and passed on in the same order in which he had come. This took an hour and was something to see. The causeway continued beyond the battlement. Before it reached the street it was interrupted by a wooden drawbridge ten paces across, under which the water flowed from one lake to the other.

Moctezuma came as far as this bridge to greet Cortés. He walked under a pallium of gold and green feathers, strung about with silver hangings, and carried by four gentlemen. He was supported on the arms of his nephews, the great princes Cuitlahuac and Cacama. All three were dressed alike, save that Moctezuma wore golden shoes set with precious stones, which were really only sandals held on by straps like those of the ancients. Servants walked ahead of them two by two, laying down and removing mantles, lest Moctezuma should tread on the ground. Two hundred lords came next, as if in a procession, all barefoot, but wearing a richer livery than the 3,000 of the first escort. Moctezuma kept to the middle of the street and the rest followed him, hugging the walls, their eyes downcast, for it would have been an act of great irreverence to gaze upon his face.

Cortés dismounted and approached Moctezuma to embrace him in the Spanish fashion, but was prevented by those who were supporting him, for it was a sin to touch him. Even so, the two men saluted each other, and Cortés threw about Moctezuma's neck a necklace of pearls, diamonds, and other gems made of glass. Moctezuma stepped forward with one of his nephews, and ordered the other to lead Cortés by the hand behind him. As they set off, the men in livery came up one by one to speak to Cortés and felicitate him upon his arrival; and then, touching the earth with their hands, they passed on and took their places as before. If all the citizens had saluted him as they wished, it would have taken the whole day; but, since the king had gone on ahead, they all turned their faces to the wall and did not dare approach Cortés.

Moctezuma was pleased with his glass necklace and, being a great prince and unwilling to accept a present without giving a better one in exchange, he at once commanded two necklaces to be brought. From each of them hung eight gold shrimps (which they greatly esteem) as large as snails and an inch long, of perfect workmanship, and he cast it about Cortés' neck with his own hands, which the astonished Mexicans considered a mark of great favor.

By this time they were approaching the end of the street, which is a third of a league long [a league is about two and a half miles—Ed.], wide, straight, and very beautiful, lined with houses on both sides; and so many people were crowded at the doors and windows and on the roofs that I know not who was the more amazed, our men at seeing such a multitude of men and women in the city, or they, at the guns, horses, beards, and dress of our men, such as they had never before seen.

The Spaniards then came to a large courtyard in what had been the house of Axayacatl [the ruler of the Aztecs from 1469–79, and the father of Moctezuma —Ed.], where idols were kept. At the door Moctezuma took Cortés by the hand and led him to a large room, saying: "You are now in your own house. Eat, rest, and enjoy yourself, and I shall return later."

Such, just as you have heard it, was the reception given Hernán Cortés by Moctezuma, a most powerful king, in his great city of Mexico, on the eighth day of November of the year of Our Lord 1519.

Moctezuma

MOCTEZUMA WAS A MAN of middling size, thin, and, like all Indians, of a very dark complexion. He wore his hair long and had no more than six bristles on his chin, black and about an inch long. He was of an amiable though severe disposition, affable, well-spoken, and gracious, which made him respected and feared. Moctezuma means a furious and solemn man. The Mexicans add the suffix *tzin* to the given names of kings, lords, and women as a mark of courtesy or dignity, as we do with *don,* the Turks with *sultan,* and the Moors with *mulei;* so they call Moctezuma *Moctezumatzin.* His people endowed him with such majesty that they would not sit in his presence, or wear shoes, or look him in the face, with the exception of only a few great lords. But he would not permit the Spaniards to remain standing, either because he enjoyed their society, or because of his high regard for them. When he took a notion to dress in the Spanish fashion, he would exchange garments with them. He changed his own four times a day and never wore the same garment twice. His used garments were saved and given as rewards and presents to servants and messengers, or, as a token of favor and privilege, to soldiers who had fought and captured an enemy. The many and beautiful mantles that he sent to Cortés were of such.

Moctezuma was naturally clean and neat; he bathed twice a day. He seldom left his chambers except to eat, and always ate alone, but gravely and abundantly. His table was a cushion or a couple of dyed skins; his chair a bench of four legs, made from one piece, the seat hollowed out, very well carved and painted. His dishes were brought in by four hundred pages, gentlemen's sons, who served them all at once in his dining hall. Moctezuma would enter and look them over, pointing to those he liked, whereupon they would be set on braziers of live coals, to keep them warm and preserve their flavor. He would seldom touch other dishes, unless it was a well-prepared one recommended by his majordomo.

Before he sat down to eat, as many as twenty of his wives would enter, the most beautiful or shapely, or those serving their weekly turn, who very humbly brought him his food, after which he sat down. Then the steward would enter and draw a wooden screen to keep the people from crowding in, and only the steward could serve him, for the pages were not permitted to approach the table or utter a word; nor could any of those present speak while their master was eating, save only his jester, or someone who had a question to ask; and all waited on him barefoot. His drinking was not done with such pomp and ceremony.

Some six old men, with whom Moctezuma would share portions of the dishes he liked, were always at the king's side, although somewhat withdrawn. They accepted the food reverently and ate it even more respectfully, not looking him in the face—which was the greatest mark of humility they could show him. During his meals he would listen to the music of pipes, flutes, conches, bone fifes, drums, and other instruments of the kind, for they have no better ones; nor can they sing, I say, because they do not know how, and their voices are bad besides.

Always present at his meals were dwarfs, hunchbacks, cripples, and so on, all for his entertainment and amusement, and these, along with the jesters and mountebanks, were given the leavings to eat at one end of the hall. Whatever else was left over was eaten by the three thousand men of the regular guard, who stayed in the courtyards and square—which is why it is said that three thousand dishes were always served, and three thousand pitchers of the beverage they drink, and that the cellar and pantry were never closed. It was a wonderful thing to see what they contained. Everything obtainable in the market was cooked and served daily without fail. There was, as we shall relate elsewhere, an infinite variety, in addition to what was brought in by hunters, tenants, and tributaries.

The plates, bowls, cups, pitchers, and the rest of the service were of very good pottery, as good as that of Spain, and were never used for more than one of the king's meals. He also had a large number of gold and silver vessels, which he seldom used, because to use them more than once would seem a low thing to do. Some have said that Moctezuma cooked and ate babies, but the only human flesh he ate was that of sacrificed men, and this not commonly. When the table linen was removed, the men and women, who were still standing, would approach to offer him water for his hands, which they did with equal respect, and then retired to their own chambers to eat with the others, as they all did, save only the gentlemen and pages who were on duty.

While Moctezuma was still seated and the table had been taken away and the people departed, the merchants entered, barefoot, for all removed their shoes upon entering the palace, save only great lords such as those of Texcoco and Tacuba, and a few of his kinsmen and friends. All came very poorly dressed: if they were lords or great men, and it was cold, they wore old blankets, coarse and tattered, over their fine new mantles. They bowed three times, but did not look him in the face, and spoke humbly, always facing him. He answered them with great dignity, in a low voice and few words. He did not always speak or answer them, whereupon they would leave, walking backward.

Then Moctezuma would amuse himself by listening to music and ballads, or to his jesters, as he was very fond of doing, or by watching certain jugglers who use their feet as ours do their hands. They hold between their feet a log as big as a girder, round, even, and smooth, which they toss into the air and catch, spinning it a couple of thousand times, so cleverly and quickly that the eye can hardly follow it. Besides this, they perform other tricks and comical acts with astonishing skill and art. . . . They also perform grotesque dances, in which three men mount one above the other, resting upon the shoulders of the bottom man, while the top man does extraordinary things . . .

The Ball Game

AT OTHER TIMES MOCTEZUMA went to the *tlachtli*, or ball court. The ball itself is called *ullamalixtli*, which is made of the gum of the *ulli* [*hule*], a tree of the hot country. This tree, when slashed, oozes thick white drops that soon harden, and are gathered, mixed, and treated. The gum turns as black as pitch, but does not stain. It is rolled into balls which, although heavy and hard to the hand, bounce and jump very well, better than our inflated ones. The game is not played for points, but only for the final victory, which goes to the side that knocks the ball against the opponents' wall, or over it. The players may hit the ball with any part of the body they please, although certain strokes [*e.g.*, with the hands] are penalized by loss of the ball.

The Spaniards are greeted by Moctezuma (right) and his notables at the gates of his capital. Between the two groups stands Marina, the young Indian woman of noble birth who became Cortés' mistress and the expedition's interpreter.

Hitting it with the hips or thighs is the most approved play, for which reason they protect those parts with leather shields. The game lasts as long as the ball is kept bouncing, and it bounces for a long time. They play for stakes, wagering, say, a load of cotton mantles, more or less, according to the means of the players. They also wager articles of gold and featherwork, and at times even put up their own bodies. . . .

Moctezuma's Women

MOCTEZUMA HAD MANY HOUSES in and out of Mexico, some for display and recreation, some for dwellings. I shall not describe them all, for it would take too long. The one where he had his permanent residence was called Tecpan, that is to say, palace. It had twenty doors opening on the square and public streets, and three large courtyards, in one of which was a beautiful fountain. It had many halls and a hundred rooms 25 to 30 feet square, and a hundred baths. It was constructed without nails, but very solidly. The walls were of stone, marble, jasper, porphyry, black stone shot with veins of ruby red, white stone, and a translucent stone [alabaster]; the ceilings, of wood, well finished and carved to represent cedars, palms, cypresses, pines, and other trees. The chambers were painted; the floors, covered with mats; the drapes, of cotton, rabbit fur, and feathers; the beds, poor and uncomfortable, being merely blankets laid over mats or straw, or mats alone.

Few men slept in these houses, but there were a thousand women—some say three thousand, counting the ladies and their servants and slaves. Of the ladies and their daughters, who were very numerous, Moctezuma took for himself those whose looks he liked; the others he gave to his servants for wives, or to other gentlemen and lords. Thus it happened, they say, that he had a hundred and fifty women with child at one time, who, persuaded by the devil, took exercises and medicines to get rid of the babies; or perhaps [they did so] because their children could not inherit. These women were guarded by many old ones, who would not permit a man even to look at them, for the king would have nothing but chastity in his palace.

The coat of arms above the palace doors (where the banners of Moctezuma and his ancestors were hung) was an eagle in combat with a tiger, its claws extended as if to capture its prey. Some say it is a griffin and not an eagle, for there are griffins in the mountains of Tehuacán that depopulated the valley of Ahucatlán by consuming the people. They base their argument on the fact that these mountains are named Cuitlachtépetl, from *cuitlachtli*, which is to say, a griffin resembling a lion. I do not now believe that there are such, for no Spaniard has seen them. . . .

The House of Feathers

MOCTEZUMA HAD ANOTHER HOUSE with many fine apartments and several galleries resting upon pillars of jasper (these cut from a single piece), opening upon a spacious garden, in which there were ten or more ponds, some of salt water for sea fowl, others of sweet water for birds of the rivers and lakes. The ponds were frequently emptied and filled, to keep the feathers clean. So many birds lived there that they overflowed the place, and they were of such different plumages and kinds that the Spaniards were astonished, for most of them they had never known or seen before.

Each species of bird was fed the things it had eaten in its wild state: if herbs, it was given herbs; if grain, maize; if beans, these and other seeds; if fish, fish, of which the ordinary ration was ten arrobas [one arroba equals twenty-five pounds—*Ed.*] a day, caught in the lakes of Mexico. They were even fed flies and other vermin, if such was their diet. Three hundred persons were assigned to take care of the birds: some cleaned the ponds; others caught fish for them; others fed them; others deloused them; others guarded the eggs; others threw out the brooders; and still others had the most important duty of plucking them. Of the feathers, rich mantles, tapestries, shields, plumes, flyflaps, and many other things were made, adorned with gold and silver, of exquisite workmanship.

House of the Hunting Birds

MOCTEZUMA HAD ANOTHER HOUSE with very large rooms and apartments which was called the bird house, not because there were more birds in it than in the first, but because they were larger, or, perhaps, being birds of prey, they were held to be better and nobler. In the many upper rooms dwelt men, women, and children who were white in body and hair from birth, and who were considered unusual to the point of being almost miraculous, so seldom did they occur. Dwarfs, hunchbacks, cripples, and monsters were also kept there in large numbers for the king's amusement. It is said even that they were broken and made crooked in babyhood as if for the glory of the king. Each of these monsters had an apartment to himself.

In the lower rooms were many cages of stout timbers: in some, lions were kept; in others, tigers; in others, lynxes; in still others, wolves. In short, there was no kind of four-footed beast that was not represented, and all for the purpose of Moctezuma's being able to boast that, however fierce they might be, he [dared] to keep them in his house. They were fed turkeys, deer, dogs, and game. In other rooms, in great eathenware jars, pots, and vessels . . . filled with water or earth, reptiles were kept, such as boa constrictors (*muslos*), vipers, crocodiles (which they call *caimanes,* that is to say, water lizards), lizards of other kinds, and such-like vermin, as well as land and water snakes, fierce and poisonous, and ugly enough to frighten the beholder.

In another apartment and in the courtyard, in cages with round perches, were kept all manner of birds of prey, such as lanners, hawks, kites, vultures, goshawks, nine or ten varieties of falcons, and many kinds of eagles, among which were some fifty a great deal larger than our red-tails. At one feeding each of them would eat a turkey of the country, which is larger than our peacock. There were many birds of each kind, and each kind had its own cage. They consumed some 500 turkeys every day. They had three hundred servants to wait on them, not counting the hunters, who were number-less. Many of these birds were unknown to the Span-iards, but it was said they were all good hunting birds, as was manifest by their aspect, size, talons, and the prey they caught. The snakes and their mates were given the blood of men killed in sacrifice, to suck and lick, and some even say they were fed on the flesh, which the lizards devoured with great gusto. The Span-iards did not witness this, but they did see the ground all encrusted with blood, as in a slaughterhouse, which stank horribly and quaked if a stick was thrust into it.

An amazing number of men were in and out of this house, caring for the birds, beasts, and serpents. The diversity of the birds, the ferocity of the beasts, and the serpents swelling with poisonous fury delighted our Spaniards, who, however, did not enjoy their frightful hissing, the hideous roaring of the lions, the howling of the wolves, the screams of the tigers and lynxes, and the yelps of the other animals, owing to hunger or per-haps to the thought that they were caged and could not give vent to their fury. And truly, at night the place was a picture of hell and abode of the devil; and so it

was, in fact, for in one of the rooms, 150 feet long by 50 wide, was a chapel thickly plated with gold and silver, all set with pearls and precious stones: agates, cornelians, emeralds, rubies, topazes, and the like. Here Moctezuma often came in the night to pray, and the devil appeared and gave him advice on petitions and requests.

Moctezuma had another building, for the storage of grain and feathers and mantles brought in as rents and tributes. It was also something to see. Above its doors was the coat of arms, or device, of the rabbit. It housed the majordomos, treasurers, accountants, secretaries, and all those employed in the management of the royal estate. All these buildings without exception had their chapels and oratories of the devil, who was prayed to for the protection of their contents. For these reasons the buildings were very large and accommodated many people. . . .

Moctezuma's Gardens

BESIDES THOSE JUST MENTIONED, Moctezuma had many pleasure houses with delightful gardens, some of medic-inal and aromatic herbs, others of flowers, roses, and sweet-smelling trees in infinite numbers. It was some-thing to make one praise the Creator to see such variety, coolness, and perfume, and the skill and delicacy with which a thousand different figures had been fashioned out of leaves and flowers. Moctezuma did not permit any vegetables or fruits to be raised in these gardens, saying it was not fitting for kings to operate farms for profit in his pleasure spots, and that it was the duty of slaves or merchants to raise such fruits. Nevertheless, and despite what he said, he did own orchards, but at a distance, which he seldom visited. Outside of Mexico he also possessed great houses in the woods, surrounded by water, with springs, rivers, fishponds, rabbit war-rens, breeding grounds, and crags and rocks where stags and deer, hares, foxes, wolves, and other such animals roamed free, in the hunting of which the Mexican gentlemen exercised themselves much and often. So many and so great were the houses of Moctezuma that they were equalled by those of few kings.

Moctezuma's Court and Bodyguard

MOCTEZUMA HAD DAILY A COMPANY of 600 gentlemen and lords to act as his bodyguard, each with three or four armed servants to wait on him, some even with as many as twenty or more, according to their rank and wealth; so altogether they numbered 3,000 (some say many more) in the palace guard. All of them were fed with the leftovers from the king's table and his rations. The servants did not retire to their quarters until he

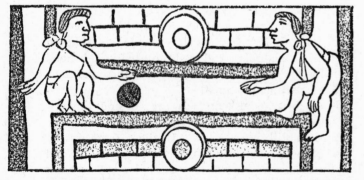

Tlachtli, *a game played with a rubber ball in an I-shaped court, was as much ritual as sport. Here Moctezuma plays another chief to determine the correctness of the latter's prediction of the downfall of the Aztecs. Moctezuma lost.*

had finished eating, and then not until night. The guard was so numerous that it quite filled the courtyards, squares, and streets [of the palace]. It could be that, to impress the Spaniards, they put on this guard and show of power, and that ordinarily it was smaller. The truth is, however, that all the lords under Mexican rule, who . . . numbered thirty, each with 100,000 vassals, resided a part of each year in Mexico at the court of the great lord Moctezuma, out of obligation and gratitude, and when they returned to their own lands and dominions, they did so with the permission and at the choice of the king. Even so, they had to leave behind a son or brother as insurance against their rebellion, and for this reason they all maintained houses in Mexico–Tenochtitlán. Such, then, were the estate and household of Moctezuma, and such was his generous and noble court.

Tributes of the King of Mexico

THERE WAS NO ONE in all his dominions that did not pay some tribute to the lord of Mexico: the lords contributing their personal service; the peasants (called *macehuales*), their persons and goods. This they did in two ways: either as renters or as owners; the owners gave a third of their yearly produce, to wit: dogs, fowl, birds of plumage, rabbits, gold, silver, precious stones, salt, wax and honey, mantles, featherwork, cotton, cacao, maize, chili, sweet potatoes, broad beans, kidney beans, and all kinds of fruits, greenstuff, and cereals, by which they live. The renters paid by the month or the year whatever they must, and because it was a great deal they were all called slaves. These, even though they had nothing to eat but eggs, yet thought the king was doing them a favor. I have heard that tributes were even assessed against their foodstuffs, and that everything else was taken from them, because of which they dressed very poorly. In fine, they possessed a single pot for cooking herbs, a stone or two for grinding maize, and a mat to sleep on. The renters and owners not only paid this tribute, but served with their persons whenever the great lord wished, although he did not call them up except for war and hunting.

Such was the ascendancy that the kings of Mexico had over them that they were silent even when their sons and daughters were taken from them for any purpose. This is why some say that, of the three children of every farmer or non-farmer, one was given for sacrifice. This is manifestly false, for in that case there would not have been a man left in the whole country, nor would it have been as populous as it was. Besides, the lords ate only the sacrificial victims, who were rarely free men, but slaves and prisoners of war. Still, they were cruel butchers, and killed during the year

many men and women, and some children, not, however, as many as some have said. . . .

All these tributes were brought to Mexico on the backs of men or in canoes, at least enough to maintain the household of Moctezuma. The other tributes were used to feed the soldiers, or were exchanged for gold, silver, precious stones, jewels, and other valuables, which the kings esteemed and kept in their apartments and treasuries. In Mexico, as I have said, there were storehouses and buildings in which the grain was kept, with a majordomo and assistants to receive it, distribute it in an orderly manner, and keep the records in picture books. Each town had its tribute collector, something like a constable, who carried a staff of authority and a fan. He listed the goods and numbers of people in the towns and provinces of his district, and brought the accounting to Mexico. If any collector made an error or cheated, he died for it, and even the members of his family would be penalized as kinsmen of a traitor to the king. Farmers failing to pay their tribute were arrested. If they were poor because of sickness, they were allowed to defer payment; if it was because of laziness, they were forced to pay. In short, if they did not fulfill their obligation and pay on the appointed days, they might be taken as slaves and sold for their debts and tributes, or even sacrificed. . . .

Moctezuma had a hundred large cities, with their provinces, from which he received the rents, tributes, homage, and vassalage I have spoken of. In some of them he maintained fortresses, garrisons, and treasurers to receive the services and taxes they paid him. His domain extended from the [Gulf to the Pacific], and two hundred leagues inland. It is true, to be sure, that in the midst of it were several provinces and large towns, such as Tlaxcala, Michoacán, Pánuco, and Tehuantepec, which were his enemies and paid him no tributes or services, but the trade he carried on with

In the era of Moctezuma—as, indeed, in modern Mexico— the outdoor marketplace with its extraordinary variety of goods and foods for sale was a busy center of Indian daily life.

them when he pleased was worth a great deal to him. There were likewise many lords and kings, such as those of Texcoco and Tacuba, who owed him nothing but obedience and homage; they were of his own lineage and were the ones to whom the kings of Mexico gave their daughters in marriage.

Mexico–Tenochtitlán

AT THE TIME OF CORTÉS' COMING, Mexico was a city of sixty thousand houses. Those of the king and lords and courtiers were large and fine; those of the others, small and miserable, without doors, without windows, but, however small they might be, seldom containing fewer than two, three, or ten inhabitants, so that the city had an infinitely large population. The main part of the city was surrounded by water. Its thoroughfares were of three kinds, all wide and splendid: one of water alone, with a great many bridges; others of earth alone; the third kind was of earth and water; I mean, they were half on land, where men could walk, and half in the water, where canoes could circulate. The waterways were naturally clean, and the streets frequently swept.

Almost all the houses had two doors, one opening on the causeway, the other on the water, where they kept their canoes for transport. The city was built upon the water, but the water was not used for drinking. Drinking water was brought in from a spring in the hill of Chapultepec, a league distant, at the foot of which were two large statues carved in the rock, of Moctezuma and (it is said) his father Axayacatl, armed with lance and shield. The water was conveyed in two pipes, each supplying an ox [a large volume] of water. When one of the pipes became foul, they used the other until it too got foul. The city was served by this spring, which also supplied water for the ponds and fountains of many houses. The water was also sold from canoes, for which certain taxes were levied.

The city was divided into two districts: one called Tlatelolco, which means island; the other, Mexico, where Moctezuma resided, which means source. It was the nobler district, for it was larger and the residence of the king. The city was known by this name, although its proper and ancient one is Tenochtitlán, which means stony fruit. . . .

Mexico–Tenochtitlán is completely surrounded by water, standing as it does in the lake. It can be approached by only three causeways: one, about half a league long, entering from the west; another from the north, about a league long. There is no causeway from the east, and one must approach by boat. To the south is the third causeway, the one by which Cortés and his companions entered, as I have said. The lake upon which Mexico is situated, although it seems to be one, is really two, very different from each other, for one is saline, bitter, and stinking, and has no fish in it, while the other is of sweet water and does have fish, although they are small. The salt lake rises and falls, and has currents caused by the winds. The fresh-water lake is higher, so that the good water flows into the bad, and not the other way around, as some have thought; it flows through some six or seven large channels cut in the causeway that separates them. These channels are crossed by some very fine wooden bridges. The salt lake is five leagues wide and eight or ten long, and is more than fifteen leagues in circumference. The fresh-water lake is about the same size, so that the whole measures more than thirty leagues roundabout. On its shores are more than fifty towns, many of them of five thousand houses, some of ten thousand, and one, Texcoco, as large as Mexico. The water that collects in this depression comes from a ring of mountains that can be seen from the city. It picks up its salt from the saline earth through which it flows. Its salinity is caused by the soil and the place, and not by something else, as many think. A great deal of salt is gathered from the lake, and is the source of a large trade.

Upon these lakes float some two hundred thousand small boats, called by the natives *acalli*, which is to say, water-houses, from *atl*, water, and *calli*, house, the word being composed from these two terms. The Spaniards called them *canoas*, a word to which they had become used in the language of Cuba and Santo Domingo. They are shaped somewhat like a trough, cut out of one piece, large or small, depending upon the size of the log. I am understating rather than exaggerating the number of these *acalli*, for some affirm that in Mexico alone there are commonly some fifty thousand of them, used for bringing in provisions and transporting people. So the canals are covered with them to a great distance beyond the city, especially on market days.

The Markets of Mexico

THE MARKET PLACE IS CALLED a *tianquiztli*. Each district and parish has its square for the exchange of merchandise, Mexico and Tlatelolco, the largest districts, having vast ones, especially the latter, where markets are held on most weekdays. . . . The market place of Mexico is wide and long, and surrounded on all sides by an arcade; so large is it, indeed, that it will hold seventy thousand or even a hundred thousand people, who go about buying and selling, for it is, so to speak, the capital of the whole country, to which people come, not only from the vicinity, but from farther off. . . .

Each trade and each kind of merchandise has its own place reserved for it, which no one else can take or occupy—which shows no little regard for public order —and because such a multitude of people and quantity of goods cannot be accommodated in the great square, the goods are spread out over the nearest streets, especially the more bulky materials, such as stone, lumber, lime, bricks, adobes, and all building materials, both rough and finished. [In the market proper] many kinds of mats are to be found, both fine and coarse; pottery of different clays and glazes, all very pretty, and every kind of vessel, from great jars to saltcellars; charcoal, firewood, and faggots; deerskins, raw or tanned, with hair or without, stained in many colors, for shoes, bucklers, shields, jackets, and coverings for wooden armor. Besides all this, there are skins of other animals: birds with their feathers still in place, dried and stuffed with straw, large and small, an astonishing thing to see because of their colors and strangeness.

The most valuable goods are salt and cotton mantles, these being white, black, and of every color, some large, some small; some designed for bed coverings, others for capes, still others for drapes, drawers, shirts, head-dresses, tablecloths, handkerchiefs, and many other things. There are also mantles of maguey fiber, palm fiber, and rabbit fur, which are good, esteemed, and worn, although those made of feathers are better. The most picturesque thing in the market is the birds: some used for food, others for their feathers, and still others for hunting. They are so many that they cannot be counted, and of such different species that I cannot name them: tame birds, birds of prey, birds of the air, land, and water. The most beautiful things in the market are the gold and featherwork, in which they make replicas of everything in every color.

The craft of the highest rank and greatest skill is that of the silversmiths. . . . They can cast a parrot that moves its tongue, head, and wings; a monkey that moves its feet and head, and holds a distaff in its hands, so naturally that it seems to be spinning, or an apple that it appears to be eating. All this was much admired by our men, for our silversmiths have not such skill. . . .

The kinds of foodstuffs sold are numberless. They will eat virtually anything that lives: snakes without head or tail; little barkless dogs, castrated and fattened; moles, dormice, mice, worms, lice; and they even eat earth which they gather with fine nets, at certain times of the year, from the surface of the lake. It is a kind of scum, neither plant nor soil, but something resembling ooze, which solidifies. It is very plentiful and a great deal of it is gathered; it is spread out on floors, like salt, and there it dries and hardens. It is made into cakes resembling bricks, which are not only sold in the market [of Mexico] but are shipped to others far outside the city. It is eaten as we eat cheese; it has a somewhat salty taste and, taken with *chil-mole,* is delicious. It is said that so many birds, attracted by the food, come to the lake in winter that they quite often cover it over in some places. . . .

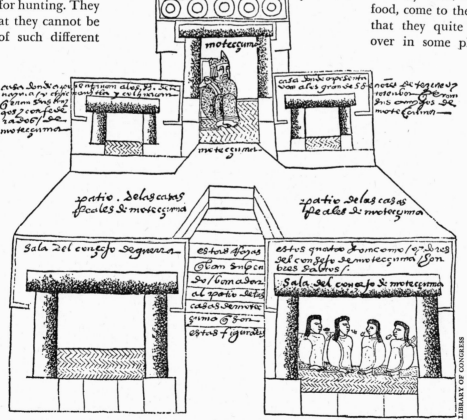

Native artists depicted Moctezuma's palace for the Codex Mendoza. The Aztec ruler is seen in his apartments (top center); in the room at lower right judges settle a lawsuit.

75

The three warriors at left carry the basic armament of the Aztec soldier —a round shield and a wooden club edged with sharp pieces of obsidian. Though the Aztec armies vastly outnumbered Cortés' tiny force, they were no match for the advanced weapons of the Spaniards. At right, the Codex Florentino depicts Indian women in their simple but richly embroidered dress. If, for the most part, they lived a sheltered existence, women could own property and follow such callings as those of midwife, priestess, and healer.

The Temple of Mexico

THE TEMPLE WAS CALLED a *teocalli,* which is to say, the house of god, the word being composed of *teotl,* god, and *calli,* a house, a very proper word if theirs had been the true God. . . . In its parishes and districts Mexico had many temples, with towers, surmounted by chapels and altars, where the idols and images of their gods were kept. These chapels were also used as sepulchers by the lords who owned them, the rest of the people being buried in the earth roundabout and in the courtyards. Since all the temples were of the same form, or almost, it will suffice to describe the principal one. . . .

The temple site was a square, measuring a crossbow shot to the side. Its stone enclosure had four gates, three of them opening on the main streets, which were a continuation of the causeways I have described. The fourth one did not open on a causeway, but on a very good street. Within this enclosure was a structure of earth and heavy stones, square, like the enclosure itself, measuring fifty fathoms to the side. As it rose from the ground, it was interrupted by great terraces, one above the other. The higher it went, the narrower became the terraces, until it resembled a pyramid of Egypt, save that it did not end in a point, but in a square platform eight or ten fathoms wide. The west side had no terraces, but a stairway leading to the top, each step of which was a good span in height. Altogether there were 113 or 114 of the steps, which, being many and high and made of handsome stone, gave the structure an imposing appearance. To see the priests climbing and descending them during some ceremony, or carrying a man up to be sacrificed, was a spectacle to behold.

At the summit were two very large altars, separated from each other, and set so close to the edge of the platform that there was hardly enough room to allow a man to pass easily behind them. One of these altars was at the right, the other at the left. They were not more than five spans in height, and their stone walls were painted with ugly and horrible figures. Each altar had a very pretty chapel built of carved wood, and each had three lofts, one placed above the other, quite high, of carved panelling. The chapels stood well above the pyramid and, viewed from a distance, gave it the appearance of a tall and handsome tower. From it one had a fine view of the city and the lake with all its towns, the most beautiful sight in the world. This was the spectacle that Moctezuma showed Cortés and the Spaniards when he took them to the top of the temple. Between the head of the stairs and the altars was a small square, but more than wide enough for the priests to celebrate their rites without crowding.

All the people prayed with their faces toward the rising sun, which is why the great temples are so placed. In each of the altars was a very large idol. Apart from the towers formed by the chapels on this pyramid, there were forty or more others, large and small, raised upon the lesser *teocallis* which surrounded the great one. These, although of the same design, did not face the east, but other parts of the sky, to differentiate them from the great temple. Some were larger than the others, and each was dedicated to a different god, one to the god of air, called Quetzalcoatl, whose temple was round, for the air encompasses the sky. Its entrance was through a door carved in the form of a serpent's mouth, diabolically painted, with fangs and teeth exposed, which frightened those who entered, especially the Christians, to whom it looked like the mouth of hell. . . . All these temples had

adjoining houses for the service of their priests and particular gods.

At each entrance of the great temple there was a large hall containing sizable chambers on its two floors. They were filled with arms, for the temples of every town were community houses and served as defenses and fortresses, which is why munitions and stores were kept in them. There were also three other halls of equal height, with flat roofs, tall and large, their walls of painted stones, the ceiling joists fancifully carved; and within, many chapels or chambers with very small doors, very dark inside, where an infinite number of idols were kept, great and small, made of many kinds of metals and materials. All of them were black with blood, for they were smeared over and sprayed with it whenever a man was sacrificed. They stank horribly, in spite of which the priests entered the chapels daily and, when they were preparing to kill and sacrifice a man, would allow no one else to enter, unless it was some great personage. These ministers of the devil had a large pond, fed by a pipe leading from the principal drinking fountain, where they washed off the blood of the sacrifices, from themselves and their robes. This pond was also used for the kitchens and the poultry. The rest of the great square was empty and open, and was used for the raising of birds, for herb gardens, sweet-smelling trees, rose bushes, and flowers for the altars.

Such, just as I have described it, was the great temple of Mexico, so vast and so strange, which these deluded men raised to their false gods. It housed continually five thousand people; all slept within it and ate at its expense, for it was very rich, having many towns whose obligation it was to build and maintain it in service.

The Idols of Mexico

THE GODS OF MEXICO, it was said, numbered two thousand. The most important of them were Huitzilopochtli and Tezcatlipoca, whose images stood upon the altars at the summit of the *teocalli*. They were of stone, of gigantic size, thickness, and height, covered with mother-of-pearl, in which many pearls, precious stones, and gold were set, held in place by a cement made of *zacotl*, decorated with mosaics representing birds, snakes, animals, fishes, and flowers, done in turquoises, emeralds, chalcedonies, amethysts, and other small stones, which made a very handsome design against the mother-of-pearl. Each of the idols wore about its waist thick snakes of gold, and each wore a necklace of golden hummingbirds, a golden mask with mirror-like eyes, and, at the back, a dead man's face—all having their meaning and symbolism. The two gods were brothers: Tezcatlipoca, god of plenty, and Huitzilopochtli, god of war, who was worshipped and esteemed above all the others.

Another very large idol stood in the chapel of the said gods which, according to some, was the greatest and best of them. It was made of all the edible and useful seeds found in the country, which were ground and kneaded with the blood of innocent babes and virgins, who had been sacrificed and their hearts offered to the idol as first fruits. The priests and ministers of the temple consecrated the idol with the utmost pomp and ceremony. The people of the whole city and country attended the consecration with incredible rejoicing and devotion, and many of the pious approached the idol after it had been blessed, to touch it with their hands and press into the dough precious stones, small pieces of gold, and other jewels and ornaments taken from their persons. After the ceremony, no layman might touch the idol or enter its chapel, not even the monks, but only the *tlamacazque*, that is, the priest. They replaced the idol from time to time and broke up the old one, and blessed were they who could obtain a piece of it for a relic and precious memento, especially the soldiers. At the time of the consecration of the idol, a flask of water was also blessed; it was piously guarded at the foot of the altar to sanctify the king when he was crowned, and to bless the captain-general when he was elected during a war, he being given some of it to drink.

The Ossuary

OUTSIDE THE TEMPLE, more than a stone's throw from the principal gate, was an ossuary built of the skulls of men taken in battle and sacrificed. It was in the form of a theatre, longer than it was wide, of stone and mortar, with its benches, between the stones of which skulls were set, teeth outward. At the ends of the theatre were two towers, built entirely of mortar and skulls, the walls of which, containing, so far as could be seen, no stone or other material, were strangely handsome. In the upper part of the theatre stood seventy or more tall poles, four or five spans apart, into which pegs had been driven from top to bottom. These pegs stood out like studs, and each of them had five skulls impaled on it through the temples. Andrés de Tapia, who described it to me, and Gonzalo de Umbria counted them one day and found them to number 136,000 skulls, including those on the poles and steps. Those in the towers could not be counted. This was a cruel custom, although it had some color of humanity, because it was a reminder of death. Certain persons had the duty of replacing the skulls that fell out, so the number did not diminish.

Moctezuma Is Arrested

HERNÁN CORTÉS AND THE SPANIARDS spent six days viewing the city and learning its secrets as well as the notable things we have described. . . . They were frequently visited by Moctezuma and the gentlemen of his court, as well as others, and were very well provided for, as on the first day. The Indian friends were also looked after, and the horses were fed green *alcacer*, a fresh grass that grows all the year round, flour, grain, roses, and everything else their masters requested, and were even bedded down in flowers.

Notwithstanding the fact that the Spaniards were so pampered and were so proud at being in such a rich country where they could fill their hands, not all of them were happy or contented, some being afraid and beset with misgivings.

This was especially true of Cortés, who, as their head and chief, had the obligation of watching over and guarding his companions. He was particularly uneasy when he contemplated the situation of Mexico, its size and numbers of people, and when he saw the anxiety of many Spaniards who came to him and told him of the fortress and web in which they were caught, for it seemed to them that not a man could escape whenever Moctezuma should take the notion, or the city should rise. It would only be necessary indeed, for each citizen to throw a stone, or break the bridges of the causeways, or cut off supplies—all of which things the Indians could easily do.

So it was that Cortés, with his anxiety to guard his men, avoid such dangers, and surmount any obstacles in the path of his desires, decided to arrest Moctezuma. . . . The opportunity, or incident, which furthered his purpose was the death of nine Spaniards

To the Spaniards, a particularly repugnant feature of the Aztec religious ritual was human sacrifice—often accompanied by ceremonial cannibalism. In this scene, a priest wielding a stone dagger has just ripped out the heart of his victim and is offering it to the Aztec sun god, Tonatiuh.

killed by Cualpopoca.* Besides, he had boldly written the Emperor that he would seize Moctezuma and his empire. . . .

The next morning certain Spaniards, accompanied by many Indians of Tlaxcala, came to tell Cortés that the people of the city were plotting to kill him and, to ensure their success, to break the bridges over the causeways. At these tidings, true or false, Cortés left half the Spaniards to guard his quarters, posted many others at the street crossings, and told the rest to go to the palace very innocently, in twos and threes, or as they thought best, and tell Moctezuma that he must see him about matters of life and death.

They did so, and Cortés went straight to Moctezuma, concealing his weapons, as did the others. Moctezuma came out to meet him and led him to his

* In one of the coastal towns that had submitted to Cortés, the Indians refused to pay tribute to Moctezuma. When Moctezuma's tribute-gatherer, Cualpopoca, tried to back his demands with force, fighting broke out. Though Cualpopoca's men were beaten, several Spaniards—the exact number is undetermined—lost their lives. Apparently Cortés was aware of the incident long before he reached the city of Mexico—*Ed.*

reception room. As many as thirty Spaniards entered with him, while the rest remained at the door of the courtyard. Cortés greeted Moctezuma as usual, and then began to jest and banter with him, as he had done before at various times. Moctezuma, who was very easy, giving no thought to what fortune had in store for him, was cheerful and pleased with this discourse. He gave Cortés many gold jewels and one of his daughters, and gave him the daughters of other nobles for the Spaniards. Cortés accepted them to please him, because Moctezuma would have been insulted otherwise; but he told him he was a married man and could not take the girl as his wife, because under Christian law no one was permitted to have more than one, on pain of being dishonored and branded on the forehead. After all this, he showed Moctezuma the letters of Pedro de Ircio [which told of the fight with Cualpopoca and the death of the Spaniards—Ed.] and had them translated for him. In them Ircio accused Cualpopoca of having killed so many Spaniards, and accused Moctezuma himself of having ordered it done and of having ordered his men to make public that he wished to kill the Spaniards and cut the bridges.

Moctezuma denied both charges, saying it was a lie on the part of his vassals and a very great falsehood that the wicked Cualpopoca had perpetrated against him. To prove to Cortés that this was the truth, in his great rage he called certain of his servants there and then, and ordered them to bring Cualpopoca before him, giving them a jewel from his arm as a seal, carved with the figure of Huitzilopochtli. The messengers left at once, and Cortés said to him: "My lord, it will be necessary for your Highness to come to my apartment and remain there until the messengers return bringing Cualpopoca, to clear up the matter of the killing of my Spaniards. There you will be well treated and served, and will rule, just as you do from here. Be not afflicted, for I shall defend your honor and person as I would my own, or that of my King; and forgive me for this, because I cannot do otherwise. If I should tolerate your conduct, my men here would be vexed with me for not defending and aiding them. And so, order your people not to be angry or make a disturbance, and bear in mind that if any ill befalls us, you will pay for it with your life, for it lies with you whether you will keep silent and not stir up your people."

Moctezuma was profoundly shaken and said with all gravity: "My person is not such as can be taken prisoner and, even if I should consent to it, my people would not suffer it." The two spent more then four hours discussing the matter, at the end of which Moctezuma said he would go [with Cortés], because he

had to rule and govern. He ordered a room to be well furnished and prepared for him in the house and court of the Spaniards, and went there with Cortés. Many lords, barefoot and weeping, undressed him, put his clothes under their arms, and bore him off in a rich litter. When it was noised about the city that the king was a prisoner in the hands of the Spaniards, it erupted in a great tumult. But Moctezuma comforted those who were weeping, and told the rest to desist, saying that he was not a prisoner, nor was he there against his will, but much to his liking.

Cortés put a captain and a guard over him and changed the guard daily, so that there were always Spaniards to cheer and entertain him. For his part, Moctezuma greatly enjoyed their company, and always gave them something. He was served there by his own people, as in his palace, and by the Spaniards also, who put themselves out to please him, and Cortés himself brought him every kind of gift, begging him at the same time not to feel badly about it, and leaving him free to hear suits, dispatch his affairs, attend to the government of his realms as before, and to speak publicly and privately with all those of his people who wished to see him—which was the bait that caused Moctezuma and his Indians to take the hook.

Never did Greek or Roman, or man of any nation, since kings have existed, do what Cortés did in seizing Moctezuma, a most powerful king, in his own house, a very strong place, surrounded by an infinity of people, while Cortés had only 450 companions.

With Moctezuma their hostage, the Spaniards remained in the Aztec capital for another six months. But Cortés, who had never received official approval from the Crown, suddenly found himself threatened by a rival expedition of Spaniards. Leaving a garrison behind, he hastened to the coast, and forced the newcomers to submit to his leadership. Meanwhile, in the city of Mexico, his men had goaded the Aztecs into an open uprising; Cortés returned to find them barricaded in their quarters at the palace of Axayacatl. When he pushed a reluctant Moctezuma in front of his angry people, they proceeded to stone their onetime god-king and wound him mortally. Cortés now had no choice but to retreat. On the night of June 30, 1520—remembered ever after as la noche triste—*his troops fought their way out along the causeway, and only escaped with heavy losses. But by the end of the year, Cortés was back with reinforcements. One by one, the towns surrounding the Aztec capital succumbed; in May, 1521, the actual siege of the city of Mexico began. It lasted three months. On August 13, when the Spaniards finally entered the city, most of it was a smoking ruin. What little was left, they destroyed.*
— The Editors

"Fill yourself up, clean your plate"

CONTINUED FROM PAGE 64

became famous for his usefulness to the American cause. Christopher Ludwick, the city's first gingerbread baker, was commissioned by the Congress as baker general of the Continental Army. He must have been a good baker. Washington, who called him "my honest friend," often had him to dine. Somehow he kept the ovens going even at Valley Forge. After the Revolution, in which Ludwick lost his property, he built another estate from the profits of his baking and left it to be shared by all the churches of Germantown, Catholic and Protestant, and to start public schools.

This admirable citizen was also the first American on record to employ food as a weapon in psychological warfare. Learning that the British had quartered German mercenaries on Staten Island, Ludwick—who was a native of Hesse—obtained permission from Congress to go there as a secret propaganda agent. He did not discuss ideologies, in which one assumes the Germans were not much interested. Instead he told them, as Fredric Klees has written in *The Pennsylvania Dutch*, "of the wonders of Philadelphia, of the mile-long market in the High Street with counters laden with plump chickens and sausages, with crisp fresh bread and buns fragrant with cinnamon, with cherries and sparrowgrass and peas and other vegetables in season; of the snug inns where a man could sit at ease before the fire and down his pot of liquor, or turn in between fresh, lavender-scented sheets." At the first opportunity, dozens of Germans deserted to the American lines. Many of their descendants are in Pennsylvania still, but they are not usually counted among the Pennsylvania Dutch. That title is generally reserved for those who had emigrated before the Revolution and had already created this abundant fare.

Throughout the nineteenth century the life of the region changed surprisingly little. The railroad came to replace the Conestoga wagon. Lean and hungry Confederate armies invaded several times, the Southerners writing home their astonishment at such peace and plenty. In the latter part of the century, as commerce began to rival agriculture in importance, many of the Reformed and Lutheran families began to move to town. But many others, along with nearly all the Plain People, stayed on the farm. No group of Americans has ever loved the land more intensely. (One of them asked to be buried standing up so that he could still "look over his farm," and his strange grave, topped by a small brick arch, is still to be seen near Collegeville.)

Well into the twentieth century these farms were still food factories such as have never been excelled, and their housewives became celebrated in verse:

> She stews and she fries,
> She makes pumpkin pies,
> She shines pot and pan,
> She darns for her man,
> She sews and she knits,
> Dries cherries and schnitz.

One historian of the region, J. George Frederick, has documented the legend in detail, from his memories of his grandparents' farm in the 1880's. His grandmother bought almost nothing from the store except sugar, salt, pepper, and coffee. From clay on their farm they even baked their own earthen pots, crocks, and pie plates—in the winter, when farm work was light. Every day after milking, of course, there was cream to be separated by hand. Making butter and cheese went on steadily and so did baking. The oven, in this home as in most, stood outside the house. It was breast-high, fired by loads of brushwood burned to ashes, which were then raked out. Loaves of bread, pies, cookies, and crumb cakes were placed on the hot brick hearth, and when these were done the remaining heat was used for drying fruit.

In the spring there was a big garden to plant, allowing a surplus for the market. Dandelions were made into wine, and raspberries and blackberries were picked for pies or for drying. For most of the year fruit was constantly being dried, in the sunshine or in the oven. From these dried fruits the Pennsylvania Dutch baked probably the world's greatest variety of pies the year round. But the universal favorite, of course, was *Schnitz* (a German word meaning "cut"), which is dried apple slices and which even today is still among the basic facts of life in Pennsylvania Dutch country. ("What do I get if I slice an apple in half?" asks the arithmetic teacher. "Halves," the children reply. "And if I slice the halves?" "Quarters," they say. "And if I slice the quarters?" "SCHNITZ!" cry the children.)

Schnitz, which was also used as chewing gum before the arrival of the store-bought variety, is even on the map. A farmer on his way to market once upset a wagonload in a creek; the slices swelled up in the water to flood the whole valley, and today this is Schnitz Creek.

One of the busiest fall activities among the Pennsylvania Dutch was the storing of vegetables for the winter: beets, turnips, potatoes, and pumpkins. Mr. Frederick's grandmother took prizes for pumpkins at the county fair. Before frost she cut off the best, leaving a tail of vine which she stuck in a jar of milk, through which the thirsty pumpkin continued to grow. Fall was also the time for gathering chestnuts for stuffing fowls, and walnuts for pickling or cookies. And of course sauerkraut was made in the autumn. An unnamed Pennsylvania Wordsworth once sang:

> *All my soul is in delight*
> *When mommy fixes kraut just right.*

Kraut, in the early days, was made by men who "stomped" the cabbage with their bare feet, like peasants pressing grapes for wine. It is now, of course, made by quite sanitary methods, and the Pennsylvania Dutch, who adore it, try to give it an aristocratic background, pointing out that it was reputed to be the favorite food of Charlemagne. It is, in any case, a favorite of theirs. And it is best accompanied by pig meat. The home-grown poet quoted above continued:

> *Calm my troubled, sinful mood—*
> *Oh, but pork is always good!*

He had ample nourishment for his spiritual aspirations after hog butchering and meat packing on the farm early in December. For this season the men of the family joined the food factory. They brought in specially selected woods for the smokehouse, each chosen to give the best flavor to sausages, tongues, bacon, pork, and ham. (Pennsylvania Dutch country smoked ham was perhaps the inspiration for the saltier "country hams" of the South, for the Dutch early began to spread from Pennsylvania down through Maryland and the valleys of Virginia deep into the southern mountains, where they are found today.) Nobody has ever made more thorough use of the pig, not even the great meat-packing houses. The feet, of course, were put up in jelly, and the boys even saved the hog bristles, which they were allowed to sell in town to buy Christmas candy. From the tiniest scraps of hog meat, unusable elsewhere, they made scrapple, one of their truly great contributions. And when the butchering was all over, each respectable family set aside some of the choicest cuts of the hogs, or perhaps some sausages or a side of bacon, as presents for neighbors who had helped or as gifts to the poor at Christmas—a time when nobody in the Pennsylvania Dutch country was allowed to be hungry.

At Christmastime, too, cookies were baked by the bushel in every home; the treasured old cooky cutters, shaped like animals, had come over from the Old World. Also made for Christmas were sandtarts, doughnuts, *Lebkuchen* (a honey cake usually containing almonds, citron, or orange peel), and mince pies—called Christmas pies. The Moravians, those highborn cousins of the Pennsylvania Dutch who were finally settled by Count Nikolaus Ludwig von Zinzendorf, their leader, at Bethlehem, outdid themselves at Christmas. They erected a four-sided structure on tables to form a cooky pyramid—a forerunner of the Christmas tree, which the Pennsylvania Dutch introduced to this country.

The first Christmas tree of record appeared in the upper Rhineland in 1608; for two centuries thereafter it remained a custom in this region of Germany, whence it was brought by the emigrants to America. An issue of the *Saturday Evening Post* for 1825 described what a lovely sight the trees made, hung with cookies and candies, glimpsed through Philadelphia windows. Such jollifications were not usually the doings of the stern Plain People. It was mostly the gay Dutch who—at a time when Puritan sentiments predominated in this country and the great festival was largely ignored—made the American Christmas merry. Until the twentieth century, in fact, one day was hardly enough. They celebrated the day after, too. In the towns of the gay Dutch, Second Christmas was even livelier than Christmas Day. The local hotel might serve free drinks all day, there would be greased-pig races and shooting matches, fireworks, a cannon might be fired, and Santa Claus—who is partly a Pennsylvania Dutch invention—might arrive from a neighboring town on a special train.

Special foods followed the cycle of the Christian year. For example, doughnuts called fastnachts were prepared in abundance for Shrove Tuesday, a day when even the women ceased work. (To sew on Shrove Tuesday, some believed, might sew up the hens and keep them from laying eggs.) The fastnachts—still baked in large quantities at this season—might be round or square, and a hole in the middle was optional. But they were very powerful medicine. The last person out of bed on Shrove Tuesday morning was called the Fastnacht; he had to do extra chores and was teased and tormented about it all day long. If you wanted to grow large heads of cabbage it was essential to eat lots of fastnachts. And the lard in which they were fried was kept to heal sores or grease wagon wheels.

Ash Wednesday, of course, was not a feast day (ashes were scattered over garden and livestock), but with the approach of Holy Week many preparations had to be made. Dandelion greens had to be gathered to be eaten as a salad on Maundy Thursday, sometimes called Green Thursday. (The favorite dressing was a hot cream gravy made with bacon, and if this sounds strange for use on a green salad the only advice can be to try it.) The dandelion salad would help to keep fevers away all year, and in fact its vitamins were good to have at this season. But the great culinary activity centered around eggs.

The Pennsylvania Dutch introduced the Easter egg and its proud parent, the Easter bunny. (To make the point entirely clear they used to bake a big cooky rabbit in the act of laying an egg, until the squeamish objected.) All winter long, housewives had been saving red onionskins and other natural dyes. For a fancy design, eggs could be boiled in tightly wrapped flowered calico. Each worshipper at the Moravian Easter service received an egg marked "The Lord is Risen."

Eggs were important all week long. An egg laid on Good Friday was a real treasure and could advantageously be eaten on that day and its shell saved to drink water from on Easter morning. On that day, as soon as the children had found the bunny's nest, eggs appeared in enormous quantities. Some were made into "Easter birds"—charming, toothpick creatures; others were stuck on an Easter-egg tree. But most were eaten. Boys meeting on the street "picked eggs"; that is, each would thump his hard-boiled egg, at the base, against the other's. The egg with the weaker shell would crack and be claimed and eaten by the winner.

The Easter egg and the Christmas tree will no doubt always survive (along with Santa Claus, if he can be rescued from the Chamber of Commerce). But most of the holiday customs which the gay Dutch introduced with their feasts have long since disappeared. And looking ahead, it seems clear that it is their more self-denying relatives, the Plain People, who will do most to keep alive the Pennsylvania Dutch cuisine in its full glory for generations to come.

The Amish, in particular, make it part of their religion to farm. They are not allowed, except under rare circumstances such as physical disability, to earn their livelihood in any other way. With a tenacious judgment—and it is hard to see how they are mistaken—they realize that if their way of living is to survive, it must almost totally exclude the twentieth century. They discourage educating their children above the eighth grade and prefer them to attend their own one-teacher schools with a privy in the yard. They have no telephones in their homes, indeed no electricity at all, and use no tractors on their land. ("The tractor, it don't give

no manure.") It is almost unheard-of for an Amish family to purchase food from the store. Frozen foods would not keep, and no Amish housewife would think of feeding her man "outen a can." Their own products are far better anyway. Just as in the old days, an Amish farm is a food factory, preparing good foods the whole year through. Any surplus will bring a good price from "the fancy" at a farmers' market.

To enforce their separateness from the world, the Amish will not only excommunicate a backslider but "shun" him completely—even in the marital relationship. (It was over the necessity for this stern point of discipline that the Amish separated from the other Mennonites in Switzerland, some 270 years ago.) However, they have other, more genial methods for helping each generation in turn to keep in the old paths. A newly married couple, for example, will not take a wedding trip "into the world," but will embark in their buggy on a series of honeymoon visits throughout the neighborhood. In each house they are made welcome and feasted, and from each housewife in turn the bride learns more and more of the arts which go into preparing a feast. In Amish hands the old-fashioned Pennsylvania Dutch cuisine should be safe for many years to come.

Yet it is only fair to say that, as of this writing, many gay Dutch still cherish this heritage too. A few miles north of Lititz, for example, a venerable log tavern can be found filled with neighborhood families eating nothing but Pennsylvania Dutch food and drinking beer, both in substantial amounts. A visitor will be warmly welcomed and invited to come back next day for an "all-day raffle." (The prizes will be live turkeys and Black Angus cattle, the price of one dollar will include raffle ticket, Dutch soup, and free beer with eggs pickled in beet vinegar.) And in a store window a sign advertising a church fair recommends, "Bring container to take home soup." Such soups there will be! Corn soup with popcorn floating on top, pretzel soup, calf's-liver soup, pea soup "thick enough to stand on."

This is still a country of abundance, where good people make good food and lots of it.

Archie Robertson, formerly an information specialist for the government, is editor of The Lamp, *published by the Standard Oil Company of New Jersey, and author of* Slow Train to Yesterday *and* That Old Time Religion. *His article on Pennsylvania Dutch cooking will form one chapter of* The American Heritage Cookbook and Illustrated History of American Eating & Drinking, *to be published in August (see page 65).*

papers, waiting for no imperial sanction, invested the former senator with this badge of nobility at once.

It was June before the Doctor finally sailed from Southampton, and the Civil War had entered its bloodiest phase. Grant was clawing his way toward Richmond, while Lee and his armies performed prodigies of resistance. The Battle of the Wilderness had unfolded in May; the slaughter at Cold Harbor almost coincided with Gwin's departure. The Confederates were being driven toward defeat, but they had not lost heart or hope. One straw at which Jefferson Davis still clutched was recognition by England and France—and if those nations would not admit the Confederacy's sovereignty, then recognition by some government, somewhere. Could that be obtained, the wherewithal to go on fighting might flow into southern ports, and the North's will to continue the struggle might be broken.

Maximilian seemed to offer such an opening. Although Washington sternly refused to accept his upstart Empire and recalled its minister to Mexico, President Davis had appointed an envoy to the new court, General William Preston of Kentucky, even before Maximilian and Carlota had landed. Preston set out at once, and at Havana encountered an old friend, Doctor Gwin, on his way to Veracruz. Preston reported their conversation in a private note to Davis on June 28, 1864; in this the southern complexion of the settlers Gwin proposed to draw to Sonora was made clear.

"Doctor Gwin . . . has identified himself with the new Empire," Preston advised the Confederate President, "and has just gone on to Sonora to undertake its colonization under flattering auspices. . . . It is expected that fifteen or twenty thousand colonists thoroughly acquainted with mining can be procured from Southern men in California. . . ."

Gwin continued the journey to Mexico City. There the French ambassador, Montholon, took him at once to meet General Bazaine. The General, a pudgy little man who had proved adept at guerrilla warfare in Algeria, accepted the letter Gwin brought from Napoleon but, fearing open negotiations, insisted on a secret interview. When that first clandestine meeting was held soon after, the Doctor speedily gathered that a serious estrangement existed between the French army and the civilians, both Mexican and European, who surrounded Maximilian.

Bazaine approved Gwin's project and promised military support, but hinted at unforeseen difficulties. He did not wish to discourage the Doctor, he said—in fact, Bazaine might command the expedition into Sonora himself; but the Doctor would be well advised to have no communication with the Mexican authorities. Indeed, it might be better not to attempt to see Maximilian, certainly not just then, for his advisers were intensely jealous of French influence and doubtless were already poisoning his mind against any scheme emanating from the Tuileries.

Ignoring the General's advice, Gwin requested an interview with Maximilian; he received a courteous reply saying that the Emperor was setting out on a trip through the interior, but would receive him upon his return. Like Bazaine, Maximilian seemed to be stalling for time.

Before leaving France, it seemed, Maximilian had demurred at signing a treaty that would place Sonora under the protection of France for fifteen years in return for payment of a royalty on all metals mined there. This was a prerequisite for Gwin's operations: since he would be dependent upon French military protection against the Indians, the area must be firmly under France's control. Maximilian's scruples against signing such a treaty "in a hurry" had nettled Napoleon, but, impatient to get his puppet emperor started toward America, he waived the signing temporarily.

Upon arriving at the seat of his Empire—a remote, half-primitive, half-sophisticated city high in the mountains—Maximilian found his Mexican advisers dead set against Gwin and his scheme. They remembered Texas, and the war of 1846, when they had lost half their territory to voracious Yankees: and they grumbled that Gwin's settlers would simply take over Sonora. Too, they hinted that Gwin's secret intention was to foment a war between Mexico and the United States, to the advantage of the Confederacy. Maximilian was susceptible to these insinuations. To escape this and the many other dilemmas he faced, the Emperor set out upon a royal progress through the countryside, viewing ruins and practicing taxidermy.

Meanwhile, in Mexico City, the Doctor practiced patience. Though Maximilian had gone a-gadding, the Empress remained in the capital, and Gwin enlisted her support; he was encouraged to find her more capable and clear-headed than her airy-minded husband, and in letters to his family in France he evinced no loss of confidence.

. . . I prepared the argument in favor of the policy [he wrote], and Montholon the treaty. Mr. Corta [Napoleon's fiscal agent in Mexico] read them at large to her Majesty. The work was all well done. General Bazaine, although approving all, stood aloof, so that if the Emperor and Empress refused to make the treaty he might not be embarrassed. . . . The last time I saw him, I said I was "getting tired of inaction, and believed if he would furnish me with an outfit and an escort, I would join the army *en route* for Sonora between Durango and Mazatlan." He agreed to furnish me with everything I wanted at once, but advised me to wait, and go with him. . . . In fact, the roads are now impassable everywhere. There have not been such rains for years. . . . I must, therefore, wait on the seasons. If the treaty is made I shall be fully repaid for the delay. I am more and more satisfied, as I collect information, of the enormous richness of the gold and silver mines of Sonora, and that the climate is the most healthy and delicious.

Maximilian returned to his capital, and Gwin awaited a call to discuss business; instead, he received an invitation to a wedding. Julia, daughter of the Marquis de Montholon, was the bride, and although her Parisian wedding gown was stuck in the mud somewhere between Veracruz and Mexico City, the Emperor decreed that the wedding should be celebrated forthwith; he and Carlota stood as sponsors of the bridal pair.

During the nuptial mass Gwin was placed close to the imperial couple, in a position to study them carefully; his impression was favorable, he wrote to his daughter, though his verdict on Maximilian was tepid: "very polite, kind, and amiable"—hardly the essential qualities for a ruler.

The sociable Doctor was treated to another picturesque spectacle during October, an alfresco military mass celebrated in the camp of the French army. In his account to his family he told of being welcomed in the camp by Bazaine, who had just been made a marshal of France and was infatuated with his new honor.

As I walked among the little Frenchmen, they looked at me with curious eyes, as if they thought me a giant [Gwin recounted]. Upon the arrival of the royal cortege, the Emperor and Empress were properly received and escorted to their tents. Shortly afterwards they both came out and walked about admiring the prospect. She ran about with evident delight, like a schoolgirl on a holiday . . . dinner was soon announced. Three bands of music played at intervals during the repast, which lasted about two hours. . . .

Just as day broke, the next morning, I was aroused by the most heavenly music I ever listened to. The three bands were playing a solemn anthem . . . preparatory to the celebration of mass. When the music ceased everybody was in motion, and we all began to wash and dress right out in the open air, Emperor and all. . . . We were soon dressed, and the bugles on all sides of us called the troops into ranks. Officers galloped rapidly about, and in a short time the whole of the army had assembled around the altar, where mass was to be celebrated. . . .

It was very imposing, with the bands playing and the troops presenting and grounding arms at given signals.

After it was over, the Emperor and Empress stepped into their carriage and drove slowly off . . . at eleven o'clock, we sat down to breakfast with the Marshal, his staff, and principal officers. It lasted nearly two hours. I sat on the Marshal's right, and the theme during the whole meal was Sonora. The Marshal, it seemed, wished his staff and officers to hear me on this subject, and they were enthusiastic when he said he might take them all there. . . .

But social amenities did nothing to forward the Doctor's plans. Maximilian remained friendly, but no word of business escaped the imperial lips. Bazaine, swaggering and sly, offered excuse after excuse for not putting the Sonora expedition in motion, while Gwin awaited some sign from Paris.

Worse yet, the progress of the war in the United States was more and more disquieting, and as the year drew to a close it seemed inevitable that the Confederacy would crumble. In November, Lincoln had been re-elected President, while Sherman in Georgia and Grant in Virginia were smashing the South's last defenses. Should the North be victorious, Gwin suspected that Maximilian might shy away from the Sonora project for fear of angering Washington. Time was running out; Napoleon must act. Convinced that no one could present the impending danger as forcefully as himself, Gwin sailed for France early in January, 1865.

By this time Napoleon had become disillusioned with his Mexican glory hunt. In Europe, events had moved toward a crisis since Prussia's seizure of the Danish provinces of Schleswig and Holstein, and there was a popular outcry among the French against the ruinous expense of maintaining the army in Mexico. As his disenchantment grew, Napoleon flirted with the temptation to liquidate the whole affair, providing French pride could be saved. Trial balloons were lofted. Thus, on February 8, while Doctor Gwin was at sea, the United States consul general in Paris, John Bigelow, read in the court newspaper, the *Moniteur*, that "all reports circulating in the journals relative to a cession made to France by the Mexican government of certain provinces of Sonora, Chihuahua, etc., etc., are absolutely unfounded." Seward had been prodding Bigelow to ferret out Gwin's objective in Mexico; might it not be, suggested the Secretary of State, to create a refuge there for unregenerate Confederates—or perhaps to provide a foothold for a Confederate government in exile?

Bigelow forwarded the *Moniteur* extract with this note: "Last evening at the palace . . . before the opening of the ball, His Majesty said to me, 'I am sorry those reports got into the journals about Sonora; there is nothing whatever in them.' . . . His Majesty

When Napoleon III ordered the withdrawal of his Mexican expedition, Carlota went to Paris to beg a reprieve. On the verge of madness, she reported to Maximilian that "he curtly refuses, and no power can aid us, for he has hell on his side. . . ." In this contemporary etching, however, her farewell to Napoleon and Eugénie seems the picture of mutual esteem.

then added laughingly, 'What I want is to get out of it altogether.' "

Gwin reached Paris about March 6—and found Morny, his mainstay, desperately ill, unable to receive visitors. On March 10, the Duke died.

With this prop knocked out, the whole edifice of Gwin's hopes threatened to topple. Yet Napoleon might still save the project. Gwin obtained an audience, and, determined that the Emperor should understand the catastrophe building up in Mexico, he employed language seldom heard by emperors. Maximilian he described as an honest man, well-intentioned, a patron of the arts, a connoisseur of painting—"but of all men living, probably the least qualified to govern Mexico." He squandered his annual salary of a million and a half dollars on pageantry, while the people perished of famine; he surrounded himself with guards gorgeously caparisoned, while every highway teemed with beggars and brigands; he had produced nothing but blunders, and had brought nothing except more discord into a country already hopelessly divided. In sum, said Gwin, Maximilian was "a paper emperor," and should be dealt with as such: he must be told to approve the Sonora treaty, and Bazaine must be compelled to take the field. Further delay would mean disaster.

Napoleon replied that whatever Maximilian's shortcomings might be, he was an emperor and must be accorded respect. However, he added, the Doctor was correct in maintaining that the mineral wealth of northern Mexico should be tapped; and he requested Gwin to redraft the colonization scheme on a broader, more ambitious scale, to take in not only Sonora but such surrounding territory as might be advantageously included.

An imperial request is a command; Gwin submitted the enlarged plan, and the estimates of potential gains rekindled Napoleon's languid enthusiasm. Pledging all necessary military assistance, he urged Gwin to hasten back to Mexico. Rendered doubly cautious by past experience, Gwin put his terms on record. In a letter to Napoleon dated March 25, he stated categorically: "I am willing to return to Mexico, to put my plan of colonization into operation, provided the French troops occupy the State and aid me in my enterprise." To fortify the Emperor in his resolve, Gwin stressed anew that the "right sort" of colonists in Sonora would provide a bulwark against armed intervention by the United States; he made clear that by the "right sort" he meant southerners and their political allies.

On March 31 Napoleon provided Gwin with a letter of endorsement dictated by himself, written on the embossed stationery bearing the imperial crown and the initial "N," and signed by the Emperor's chief of cabinet, Conti.

Armed with this, Gwin left Paris about April 1, and John Bigelow—now the United States minister to France—posted a "very confidential" warning to Secretary of State Seward to take the threat of southern colonization of Sonora seriously: "I understand that Gwin has obtained the promise of the Emperor to furnish him as many soldiers as he requires. . . ."

This message was written on April 19, 1865—ten days after Appomattox, and five days after the assassination of Abraham Lincoln.

On Gwin's second trip to Mexico, his son accompanied him. They found the Empire's capital in turmoil, shocked by the hue and cry being raised in Washington against all who sympathized with the side that had "killed Lincoln." Gwin took up quarters at the Hotel Iturbide, where, gloomy and perplexed, he wrote to his wife—still in Paris—on May 11:

We arrived here at a fearful crisis in the affairs of this continent. Everything is shaken here, as elsewhere, by the surrender of Lee, and the death of Lincoln. . . . This country is paralyzed by the news. The Liberals are rejoicing at the prospect of the speedy appearance of the Yankees to exterminate the Empire and restore them to power. . . . Marshal Bazaine, aged fifty-five, is soon to be married to a mature damsel of seventeen. There is much fun made of this marriage, but I fear it will not be fun to those who want business transacted in the Empire. The time spoken of for the marriage is just the time the Marshal should be on his way to Sonora. With the Marshal courting, and the Emperor wandering through the country stuffing birds, public business is at a standstill.

Publicly the Doctor appeared sanguine, and his air of confidence led the Mexican correspondent of the New Orleans *Times* to make positive predictions in his June newsletter. "The Confederates still continue to flock to Mexico," this observer reported.

There is no doubt Doctor Gwin will get his project through. It only awaits the signature of Maximilian to become a law. He goes out as director general of emigration for the States of Sonora, Chihuahua, Durango, and Tamaulipas, with extraordinary powers and eight thousand French troops to back him. The emigration is to be strictly Southern, or Confederate. Ten thousand Confederates are to be armed and paid by the empire, but kept in the above-mentioned States as protection to the emigrants on the frontier. . . . The Southerners are elated, and golden visions float before them. . . .

But already Gwin's few remaining hopes were being clouded not only by events on the highest level of diplomacy, but by subterranean intrigues.

While travelling from Mexico City to the United States under a safe-conduct pass, a certain Colonel Don Enrique A. Mejia, who was a member of the Liberal (*juarista*) party—with friends in Maximilian's camp—was arrested at Veracruz by French military authorities and his papers seized. After eight days he was released, the papers restored, and he was politely told he might continue his journey.

Upon examining the returned papers, the Colonel found several that had not been among them before. These included two letters written by Doctor Gwin and his son, addressed to Mrs. Gwin at Paris, under cover of an outer envelope addressed to Messrs. Van den Broeck et Cie., Rue de la Chaussée d'Antin—Gwin's Paris bankers. There was also a letter signed "Massey," addressed to the "Hon. B. Wood," editor of a paper that had vigorously opposed the late war, the New York *Daily News,* and brother of the notorious Copperhead and former mayor of New York, Fernando Wood.

Leslie's Illustrated, MAY 27, 1865

A TIMELY WARNING.

Escaped Southerner—"*The Yanks have nabbed old Jeff. You had better look sharp or they'll nab you, Max.*"
Max—"*Mein Gott—I am all ready for de start.*"

The prospect of Yankee intervention in Mexico was clearly hinted at in this cartoon published soon after Appomattox.

Almost certainly these documents had been planted by someone who wished to sabotage Gwin's Sonora venture; if so, they produced the desired effect. Upon reaching Washington, Colonel Mejia handed the letters to the *juarista* minister, Matías Romero, who passed them along to Secretary of State Seward. The Secretary read them, ordered Ben Wood arrested on charges of sedition, and dictated urgent instructions to Bigelow in Paris to lodge a vigorous protest with the government of Napoleon III.

The elder Gwin's letter, undated but obviously written about the middle of May, soon after his return from France, was emotional, for in view of the South's disaster Sonora now appeared to offer his best, if not his sole, chance of political and even personal survival.

My dearly beloved Wife and Daughters, [he had begun]. The startling news from the United States has made the blood of every Southern sympathizer run cold with horror. No one will be safe in our native country. How I thank Providence that I have cast my lot elsewhere, and that very soon I will have a home for my wife and children where they will be safe from oppression, and where we have every prospect of immediate and permanent prosperity. My policy is on every man's lips as the only one that will save this Empire. The Emperor remains unaccountably away from the capital, but his minister having charge of this matter considers it so pressing that he has gone to him with it more than a week ago. . . . The delay is unpleasant, but the certainty of success that will follow . . . is a great consolation, especially when everything is so dark for us everywhere else. Never have a doubt of my success. I have less now than ever.

The intercepted letter to Ben Wood, signed "Massey," proved to be from a disaffected American, Doctor Thomas C. Massey, whom Maximilian's government had empowered to open agencies for the recruiting of emigrants for Mexico. "You see I have been cautious but positive about Dr. Gwin," his letter read. "They have *all they want* from the French Emperor. . . . *Marshal Bazaine* has certain orders anyhow; the thing will be carried out, and Gwin will go out as 'Directeur-Général, etc.' . . . There are fortunes in it, and a very peculiar kind of colonization permitted. . . ."

Behind Seward's order to Bigelow to remonstrate with the Tuileries lay the Secretary's desire to avoid hostilities with Mexico. Lee's surrender at Appomattox had determined that both Maximilian and the French must clear out, but Seward believed diplomatic pressure—backed by the postwar military might of the United States—would accomplish this without fighting. Yet General Grant was massing troops on the Texas border, and a clash might be precipitated at any moment. Seward told Bigelow to move swiftly and firmly.

On August 1, 1865, Bigelow addressed a strongly worded protest to Napoleon's foreign minister, Edouard Drouyn de Lhuys, accompanied by copies of the intercepted correspondence—which, Bigelow said, plainly showed that "Dr. William M. Gwin and family, although citizens of the United States, are disloyal to its government." Gwin's Sonora scheme, he complained, envisaged large-scale emigration "from parties in rebellion against the United States," and the ex-Senator and his associates were assuring both Napoleon and Maximilian that "their contemplated proceedings . . . will inure to the injury of the United States." Moreover, they claimed to have the French Emperor's promise of military support. This posed a threat of such gravity, the Minister said, that he had been instructed "frankly to state that the sympathies of the American people for the Republicans of Mexico are very lively, and that they are disposed to regard with impatience the continued intervention of France in that country; that any favor shown to the speculations of Dr. Gwin by the titular Emperor of Mexico, or by the imperial government of France will . . . be regarded, perhaps justly, as importing danger to the United States. . . . It is unnecessary . . . to say," the note closed, "that, having expelled the insurgents from our own borders, the United States could not look with satisfaction upon their reorganization . . . on the opposite bank of the Rio Grande. . . ."

All this was extremely embarrassing to the potentate in the Tuileries. He had been caught assisting a conspiracy against the peace and security of the United States, in violation of his solemn pledge to observe neutrality in the American conflict. A protest of such dimensions could not be ignored, and on August 7, Drouyn de Lhuys returned a peevishly phrased acknowledgment of the American minister's "mention of some plans for the colonization of Mexico deemed to have been conceived with intentions hostile to the government of the United States. It is not for me to enlighten you concerning the speculations of such and such a person who has emigrated to Mexico," Napoleon's spokesman rejoined. "But what I know of the intentions of the Mexican government enables me to say that it proposes to let the emigrants from the Southern States enter upon its territory only individually and without arms. They . . . will be immediately dispersed through the provinces of the empire and bound to abstain in their conduct from anything which might awaken the just susceptibility of neighboring nations."

Convinced he had hit the bull's-eye, Bigelow abstained from further communications during the rest of August. But on the thirty-first he had a long interview with Drouyn de Lhuys and reported the conversation in a confidential dispatch to Seward. The French minister, Bigelow said, had explained that the Tuileries resented not the American protest, but the imputation of being somehow accessory to "conversations . . . between Gwin, the Emperor, and General Bazaine which could never have occurred." True, the Emperor had seen the Doctor "two or three times, as he sees all persons who are specially acquainted with any subject in which he is interested," and Drouyn de Lhuys himself had seen Gwin twice; but he denied that there were "any engagements whatever of the character referred to with Dr. Gwin."

Although he did not know it, Bigelow was belaboring an all-but-defunct issue. His letter to Seward crossed one written by the Secretary on August 24, announcing that advices received from Mexico indicated "the schemes of Dr. Gwin and other rebel emissaries in Mexico . . . have altogether failed."

In the Mexican capital, the final act of the drama was unfolding in a champagne foam of unreality. On June 28 Marshal Bazaine had married his pretty heiress, Doña Josefa Peña, with all the panoply the capital could muster; the Emperor and Empress attended. (Exchanging court gossip with Eugénie, Carlota wrote that the Marshal was really smitten, for he had taken up dancing again and boasted he never missed an *habanera*!) The festivities were prolonged for weeks, and effectively distracted Bazaine from all thought of martial exploits. Maximilian let affairs of state glide along while he devoted his energy to pet projects like establishing an academy of sciences and attempting to assemble the portraits of all the rulers of Mexico back to Moctezuma. Meanwhile, the Sonora treaty continued to gather dust.

The Doctor's enemies at court grew bolder, and a rumor percolated through the capital that Gwin was not backed by Napoleon at all. Even as Bazaine was prancing toward the bridal bed, the government journal *El Diario del Imperio* officially sealed this rumor by publishing a repudiation of Gwin and all his schemes. Indignantly the Doctor hunted out Bazaine, who knew the truth, and urged the Marshal to exact a retraction by *El Diario*. But the bridegroom-warrior shrugged that Napoleon was involved personally, and he would not presume to meddle.

Gwin realized at last that his plan had been scuttled once and for all. Even his life was no longer safe: the *juaristas* would be delighted to shoot him, while the intriguers around Maximilian would be relieved should he be eliminated by some timely accident. There was no choice but to try to make his peace with the United States—if not for his own sake, then for his family's future.

Happy to behold the troublesome Doctor departing, Bazaine provided a military escort to convoy Gwin safely through the bandit-infested countryside to the Texas border; late in August, he crossed the line and soon after arrived at San Antonio. Reporting to the military commandant, he requested permission to travel to New York, there to take ship for France. He was passed along to the departmental commander at New Orleans, Major General Philip Sheridan, who greeted him affably and relayed the request to Washington. Back came an order to arrest the former senator; and for eight months Gwin was confined at Fort Jackson, in the soggy jungle of the Mississippi delta south of New Orleans. No charge was preferred, and he was not told who had ordered his imprisonment, but Gwin always suspected that Seward was responsible. After the first few weeks he was allowed to have certain comforts, and upon his release in April, 1866 —still by whose order and because of what circumstances he was not told—he proceeded to New York and sailed to rejoin his family in Paris.

Meanwhile, the *juarista* forces had come to life; in January, 1866, while Gwin was still a prisoner, Napoleon, harassed by European pressures, by illness, and by increasingly acerbic remonstrances from Washington, ordered his army withdrawn from Mexico. By the time Gwin left Fort Jackson, Bazaine had started the evacuation. It sounded Maximilian's death knell.

In July, Carlota hastened to Paris and beseeched Napoleon not to desert his puppet, but the Emperor was helpless. Carlota then appealed to the Pope, piteously begging that her husband should not be sacrificed and filling the Vatican with her cries, but Pius IX could do nothing. In March, 1867, the last French troops sailed for home—where, after a brief interval, they would endure the ignominy of Sedan and Metz, witness the collapse of the Second Empire, see Eugénie and Napoleon in exile, and Bazaine tried and convicted of treason. (With the help of his young wife, however, he would escape from prison and spend the rest of his life in exile in Spain.)

Left defenseless, Maximilian botched an amateurish attempt to escape, then took the field against Juárez. At Querértaro, on May 15, 1867, he was betrayed and taken prisoner; and there, on June 19, he was shot. Carlota was not with him. Her mind had given way, and she was confined in a château near Brussels, incurably insane. It was her misfortune to live on for another sixty years; she did not die until January 19, 1927.

Gwin was more fortunate. Reunited with his family in Paris, he tasted the hectic gaiety of the foundering Empire's last years (when everything seemed to have gone awry since Morny's death), giving parties that "ex-Confeds" voted almost as sumptuous as those stately entertainments for which he had been famous in Washington before the war. In 1868 Gwin returned to the United States and lived quietly in California, where he had preserved some mining properties. So completely did he subside into obscurity that the news of his death on September 4, 1885, at the age of eighty, startled old-timers. The end came in a New York hotel while he was on a trip east, trying to promote a railroad across Nicaragua.

And what of the fabulous mines of Sonora? Had Gwin been duped, or had he duped himself, with a dream of incalculable wealth lying in that wild and lonely region? No one knows. Old records may be read in many ways, and some rich deposits of silver, gold, copper, and iron have been found. But the legend of vaster fortunes somewhere amid the forbidding crags and canyons of the Sierra Madre persists and to this day lures the solitary treasure hunter.

Lately Thomas is the author of a memorable article about the eruption of Mount Pelée, "Prelude to Doomsday," which appeared in the August, 1961, AMERICAN HERITAGE. His latest book, a biography of the nineteenth-century bon vivant Sam Ward, will soon be published by Houghton Mifflin.

For further reading: Maximilian and Charlotte of Mexico, *by Egon Corti (Knopf, 1928);* The World of Napoleon III, *by Roger L. Williams (Collier Books, 1962); and* A History of Mexico, *by Henry B. Parkes (Houghton Mifflin, 1960).*

Picture credits, pp. 10–11, bottom: Queen Victoria, Brown Brothers; others, Culver Pictures.

When Gentlemen Prepared for War

CONTINUED FROM PAGE 27

along the lines of the student camps, for business and professional men who wanted military training. They thought they could produce at least one hundred volunteers. Wood was enthusiastic. He promised to hold such a camp at Plattsburg in August if even twenty-five men should enroll.

Young Roosevelt and his friends—who later formalized and expanded their impromptu organization as the Military Training Camps Association—sent out over 15,000 applications to a selected group of businessmen, bankers, lawyers, doctors, college professors, and sportsmen. At first the response was slow, with only two or three applications a day coming in, but after Wood addressed a large group at the Harvard Club of New York in June there was a rush to apply. By August over a thousand had enrolled, and 1,300 were on hand for the camp's opening on August 10.

No funds for the new venture were forthcoming from the War Department. The recruits paid their own way—thirty dollars, which included the cost of the cotton uniform. Wood had to raise extra money to take care of such necessary amenities as screens for the mess halls. Bernard Baruch gave $10,000 and persuaded others to contribute. Wood took particular pains in the selection of his training officers. All of them were West Pointers, under the command of Major Halstead Dorey. The sergeants and the corporals were old-line army noncoms.

On the evening of August 9, 1915, the Business Men's Camp Special pulled out of Grand Central Station for Plattsburg. About half those aboard had bought their uniforms in advance and were already wearing them with all the awkward self-consciousness of recruits. Officially, these somewhat overweight men, most of them in their late thirties and early forties, were motivated by undiluted patriotism and the spirit of self-sacrifice. Actually, they felt they were off on a great adventure. To them the ponderously styled United States Military Instruction Camp—known more familiarly and readily as the Business Men's Camp—was a chance to learn man's oldest trade, to say nothing of allowing them to leave the world of banks and offices behind with full public approval. Also there was the tacit understanding that if America should enter the war, camp attendance would be the first step toward a commission.

The 1,300 men who would sign the Plattsburg roster on the following day were a well-advertised elite.

Among the political figures were John Purroy Mitchel, the mayor of New York, and his police commissioner, Arthur Woods; Pennsylvania's United States senator-to-be, George Wharton Pepper; and Dudley Field Malone, the collector of the Port of New York. Percy Haughton, Harvard's football coach, was matched by Yale's great fullback, Frank Butterworth. Episcopal Bishop James De Wolfe Perry of Rhode Island led the clerical contingent. Among the younger recruits were four Roosevelts: Ted, Quentin, Archie, and their cousin Philip, one of the tallest men in camp. From newspaper references to "millionaire rookies"—like Alexander Smith Cochran, owner of the America's Cup challenger *Vanitie*—it seemed as if the Social Register had gone into khaki for the summer. Richard Harding Davis noted that in his squad there were "two fox-hunting squires from Maryland, a master of fox hounds, a gentleman jockey from Boston, and two steeple chase riders who divide between them about all the cups this country offers." The still glamorous if no longer youthful Davis, fresh from his experiences as a war correspondent in France and Belgium, was the most noted notable at Plattsburg. Although by his own request no mention was made of him in the press, everyone was aware of his presence. He was then fifty-one years old, six years above the age limit that could no more apply to him than it could to Mayor Mitchel. Indeed the limit was elastic enough to include one Andrew Pickering of Boston, who was just short of three score and ten.

It was 5:45 in the morning when the Business Men's Special pulled into a siding beyond the permanent brick buildings of the camp. Though it seemed a strange and unfamiliar world to the new arrivals, Plattsburg was commonplace enough, an army post in the standard pattern of all such built since the Civil War. Ever since the War of 1812 there had been a small infantry detachment there, which had been expanded to regimental strength in 1890.

As the men piled off the train, sleepy but eager, they found themselves facing a long, uneven drill field edged with tansy and melilot. Beyond the field a tent-city waited for them—long rows of brown pyramids extending as far as mist-shrouded Lake Champlain, and large open-sided buildings that looked to be no more than tarred roofs on posts and that turned out to be the mess shelters. A sergeant led them to the adjutant's tent where each man paid his thirty dollars—five of which he would receive back if he did no damage to government property during the month. At

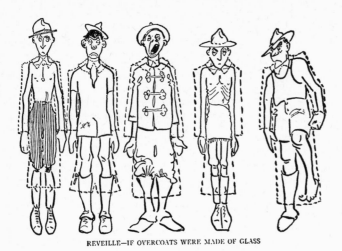

REVEILLE—IF OVERCOATS WERE MADE OF GLASS

the adjoining quartermaster's tent he received a rifle and bayonet well smeared with cosmoline, a mess kit, water bottle and cup, web belt and pack. The supply sergeant in the tent beyond issued him three blankets, a sweater, a poncho, half a pup tent, and five aluminum tent pegs. Those without uniforms were now given two pairs of olive-drab breeches, two olive-drab shirts, a pair of leggings, a cotton blouse, and a felt campaign hat with a bright braided cord.

With this overflowing armful, the recruit then stumbled across the field to the orderly tent of the company assigned to him; there the officer in charge measured his height and, according to his measurements, sent him to one of the pyramid tents that bloomed like giant mushrooms down both sides of the company street. Sixteen such streets made up the two battalions of what was now known as the Business Men's Regiment. The forty Regular officers assigned to the camp referred to their recruits as T.B.M.'s (Tired Business Men). The two hundred or so enlisted-men instructors, unable to suppress their profane amazement that anyone would pay to serve in the Army even for a month, called the eager civilians in uniform "tourists."

There were eight men to a dirt-floored tent, which was furnished with collapsible canvas cots, a lantern, a water bucket, and several tin wash basins. The newcomers set up their cots, sorted out their equipment as best they could, and tentatively essayed their uniforms. Later, in the clearing evening, they were free to explore the camp and the post beyond. Although men of affairs in their ordinary lives, now, in their temporarily adopted military life, they felt something of the uncertainty of all recruits. Regulars in their close-fitting uniforms and campaign hats with faded cords looked so very regular. The businessmen soldiers-to-be, wandering in groups past the post parade ground, were uncertain whether to salute the officers they passed or not, indeed were uncertain as to just who were officers.

Along one side of the trim parade ground stood the heavy brick lumps of the officers' quarters, duplex for the lieutenants and captains, solidly single for field officers, each marked with name and rank. In the middle distance were the equally solid two-storied enlisted men's barracks with iron-railed porches running the length of the fronts. Behind lay the stables and workshops. As these most-unmilitary recruits sauntered along the macadam walks they could see the placid lake on the other side of the parade ground, the curve of Cumberland Bay, the Green Mountains across the water to the east. It was a remarkably peaceful setting in which to prepare for war.

The recruits' first day of regular drill began at 5:55 A.M. with the staccato notes of reveille. That day was the muster pattern of the days to follow. Assembly at six and thirty minutes of calisthenics gave way, relievingly, to breakfast. After breakfast came tent-keeping and policing of grounds, rifle-cleaning, and, with first call at 7:25, the long morning of the school of the soldier. Like all recruits, the T.B.M.'s began with the elementals—the position of the soldier at attention; saluting; left, right, and about face. Then came their first fumbling attempts at the manual of arms, soft hands slapping the stocks and slings as the noncoms repeated the ancient "Hit 'em! You won't hurt the rifle!" Philip Roosevelt remarked that learning the manual of arms was like learning to tango—you kept on, and all of a sudden you found you could do it!

After forty minutes off for lunch, the newcomers slogged the hardening miles of a route march at the old army pace of three miles an hour. As time went on, such marches were varied by cross-country skirmishes over fences and ditches, past abandoned cemeteries and through swamps, with the unwary tangling themselves in poison ivy. Sometimes, with luck, there was time for a brief afternoon swim in the lake. At 5:15 P.M., the exhausted men stood in formation to the martial melancholy of the bugle sounding retreat as the flag fluttered down the mast. That daily cere-

"I want to do things in a military way," proclaims the amorous parlor snake—a Plattsburg man, of course. These drawings of what might be termed a martial fling accompanied a song, *"Give Me a Kiss by the Numbers,"* which appeared in a souvenir book put out by 1917 R.O.T.C. campers.

mony, so taken for granted by the old sweats, was to the recruits solemnly new and impressive. They were then given three quarters of an hour free until mess call. After supper there were lectures on various aspects of the military. Tattoo came at nine, call to quarters at nine forty-five, and taps at ten.

The Business Men's Camp was bounded by a thick grove of oaks and maples. At the edge of the grove, separated from the camp by a rail fence, stood a solitary pyramid tent with a flagstaff in front of it. This was the temporary quarters of the Commanding General of the East, who had come to Plattsburg for the month to watch his preparedness idea take tangible form. Every day General Wood could be seen leaning on the top fence rail watching his civilian volunteers at their drill. Often, as a substitute for their evening lectures, he talked to them informally around a campfire at a natural amphitheatre near the lake. Facing the semicircle of men as twilight faded, he spoke quietly, without rhetoric, of the military history of the United States, of preparedness, of citizens as soldiers, of the imminence of war. What he said was plain, stirring, and, above all, true. Those who attended the camps never forgot that austerely genial man with his riding crop tucked under his arm, the lines of his face etched deeply by the blaze of the logs.

For the first few days the T.B.M.'s drilled as individuals and squads, then as platoons; by the end of the first week they were drilling as companies. The following week saw them parading in battalion formation, and by its end they were ready to appear for the first time on the post parade ground as a regiment. It had taken them only days to absorb what ordinary recruits took weeks and months to learn. With these men, will and intelligence more than made up for the handicap of their years. As much to their astonishment as to that of the Regular Army instructors, they actually began to march and look and feel like soldiers. Suddenly their ordinary life of only a few days back seemed infinitely remote. From his rail fence General Wood looked at them approvingly.

To review the regimental parade, scheduled for August 25, Wood invited President Wilson, ex-Presidents Taft and Roosevelt, Secretary of War Lindley Garrison, and a number of labor leaders and university presidents. Wilson regretted that "public matters" prevented him from coming. Taft and Garrison made excuses, too, but nothing could have kept Roosevelt from Plattsburg. He accepted at once in a telegram in which he announced that he was going to make a speech to the "rookies," and asked if he might make it when the men were off duty and preferably outside the camp.

If Wood was the chief military advocate of preparedness, Theodore Roosevelt's was the civilian voice that carried farthest. Those who had enrolled in the camp acknowledged two leaders, the Colonel and the General—and it was as the Rough Rider, not as the ex-President, that Roosevelt came to Plattsburg. After the invasion of Belgium, Roosevelt had turned vociferously pro-Ally. When the *Lusitania* was sunk, he called for the immediate entry of the United States into the war against Germany. Anything less was for him the coward's part. Words did not fail him when he thought of the deedless academician in the White House penning his futile notes to Berlin. Wilson's phrase about "being too proud to fight," made only three days after the *Lusitania* went down, was for Roosevelt as contemptible as Henry Ford's remark that anyone who chose to be a soldier was either "lazy or crazy."

The ex-President disliked the President with all the scorn of a man of action for a man of the library. Wood, aware that his old friend was not likely to err on the side of tact, asked to see an advance copy of Roosevelt's speech and eliminated most of the derogatory references to the professorial Wilson. Roosevelt arrived at camp the morning of August 25, every inch the Rough Rider, wearing a wide-brimmed hat, a riding jacket of military cut, breeches, and leather leggings. He watched with field glasses while the second T.B.M. battalion worked out a tactical problem on

One!

Two!

Three!

the drill ground. In the afternoon he observed a sham battle between the first battalion and the Regulars, where the T.B.M.'s drove the enemy into the Saranac River and ended the maneuver with a bayonet charge. At the glint of steel, the Colonel showed most of his thirty-two teeth and shouted "Bully!" He was moved almost to tears at retreat when the recruits paraded as a regiment. "I have never seen a more inspiring sight," he told Wood.

At supper Roosevelt joined the rookies, many of whom he knew personally, for an old-time army meal of beans and brown bread. Afterward the whole regiment moved down to the amphitheatre by the lake to hear the Colonel's speech. The T.B.M.'s were joined there by six hundred Regulars of the post and several thousand men and women from the countryside. Colonel Roosevelt was introduced by General Wood.

Seeing the row on row of citizen-soldiers squatting attentively on the ground in front of him in the fading light, the old Rough Rider felt himself inspired. He sneered at the ignoble part the United States had played in the world for the last thirteen months. He told them resoundingly that no man was fit to be free unless he was not merely willing but eager to fit himself to fight for freedom; and he denounced "the professional pacifist, the poltroon and the college sissy."

As the light dimmed across the lake and the Green Mountains turned to gray, a lantern was fixed on a photographer's tripod and the uneven rays illuminated the Colonel's martial features. None of his hearers could possibly miss the reference to Wilson when he told them that "to treat elocution as a substitute for action, [to rely] upon high-sounding words unbacked by deeds, is proof of a mind that dwells only in the realm of shadow and of shame." Then, just as he was concluding, a half-grown Airedale wandered into the fringe of light, nudged against him, and rolled over on its back, its paws in the air, amidst much laughter from the uniformed audience. "That is a very nice dog," Roosevelt remarked, "and I like him. His present attitude is one of strict neutrality!"

Although Wood had edited out the saltier parts of the Roosevelt speech, unedited copies had been sent to the press earlier and the text was printed intact in the next day's papers. Roosevelt, waiting for the train after he had left the camp and the reservation, talked with reporters and felt free then to attack Wilson in much blunter language. On reading the accounts of the Plattsburg day, Wilson was as furious with Wood as he was with his perennial critic, Roosevelt. By the President's order the Commanding General received a sharp rebuke from Secretary Garrison, to which was added a warning against providing any further opportunity for such "unfortunate consequences," at Plattsburg or any other camp. Wood accepted the rebuke in soldierly silence. But Roosevelt's speech and Garrison's reply echoed from coast to coast. The incident stirred the public and raised preparedness to a portentous national issue.

During the latter part of their course the T.B.M.'s divided according to aptitude or physical condition into infantry, cavalry, artillery, and signals. Mornings they still drilled together, but mimic warfare more and more supplanted drill. Companies marching outside camp learned to send out Cossack posts, combat patrols, and advance and rear guards. Each man spent two days firing on the range, found out the bone-shaking way about tightening slings and squeezing triggers, came to recognize the sight of a white disk hoisted over the target's face as indicating a bull's eye, and the dismal red flag—Maggie's drawers, in newly acquired army lingo—as a clean miss. In the evening after lectures, most of the recruits would gather in their company tents to listen to the company commander elucidate the tactics laid down in Drill Regulations. At taps, when the lanterns were extinguished and the camp, except for the brown glow of General Wood's tent, lay dark, the sergeants making bed-checks from tent to tent down each company street never found a single AWOL. The T.B.M.'s were too serious, and too tired.

The climax of the Business Men's Camp came when the regiment spent nine days of war games in the field matched against Regulars. Their mock battles ranged over the Adirondack country, west as far as Dannemora, north to Chazy and Coopersville and the Canadian border. Each night the recruits pitched their pup tents at some new site. They learned to make up their packs, roll their blankets in the dark, cook a meal in a mess-tin, break camp in five minutes. Their rifles loaded with blanks, they tramped through the browning countryside, over stone walls and across fields now bright with goldenrod, always on the alert for enemy scouts and patrols identifiable by white hatbands. Already there was the first hint of scarlet in the maples, the crickets were shrill at night, and mornings the dew lay heavily on tent and poncho. In this roughing-it the men found a curious happiness, a feeling of being old campaigners at last.

Richard Harding Davis—naturally in a cavalry troop—described one of their evening bivouacs: "Back of us was a forest of magnificent pines and overhead a harvest moon. When the work was done and each man began to cook, and the hundreds of tiny fires burned red in the moonlight and were reflected in the lake, the picture was one of great beauty. Nor did the odors of frying bacon and steaming coffee in any degree spoil it."

Many of the men kept diaries and notebooks. One of them, sitting in a clump of joe-pye weed and jotting down a few lines at the edge of a field just before a bayonet charge, remarked on the serenity of the blue Adirondacks and the hard puffs of cumulus moving across the sky. "Ahead of me an officer with field-glasses," he pencilled in his book. "Three brown figures beyond wearing cartridge belts and carrying slung rifles. A whistle blows, there is a shout—and from every bush and hollow a khaki jack-in-the-box springs up rifle in hand until the long field swarms with them."

Camp ended on Saturday, September 4, at the beginning of the Labor Day weekend, the same day that Henry Ford gave a million dollars to a campaign "for peace and against preparedness." From New York had come rumors of a mustering-out parade of the Business Men's Regiment down Fifth Avenue—a gesture that would have appealed to Roosevelt but which Wood quietly and quickly shelved. When reveille sounded on the last morning there were a few moments of silence in the tent city. Suddenly the post band, assembled in secret near the camp flagpole, crashed forth with "Hail! Hail! The Gang's All Here!" With yells and cheers the T.B.M.'s

swarmed out of their tents to snake-dance after the band as it marched in and out of the company streets. The gang was all there—for the last line-up, the last mess, the last packing, and then the last look at Plattsburg.

A second course was held two days after Labor Day, but this off-season camp drew only 600 recruits. By the following summer, however, there were nine additional camps on the Plattsburg model attended by

16,000 men. Some of the original Plattsburgers who re-enrolled in 1916 received reserve commissions at the end of their course. Ted Roosevelt became a major, his brother Archie, a first lieutenant. By the war summer of 1917, Plattsburg had evolved into an officers' training camp where the "ninety-day wonders" emerged from a three-months course with gold second-lieutenant's bars on their shoulders. In the sterner light of that later training the T.B.M.'s seemed the merest play-soldiers.

Looked at in a strict military sense, the effect of the initial 1915 Plattsburg camp was negligible, the lessons learned there almost useless to the minority of T.B.M.'s who later saw active service in the First World War. Nevertheless, Plattsburg as an idea was large and compelling, surviving long after the war in the Citizen's Military Training Camps and the summer encampments of the Reserve Officers' Training Corps. (As late as 1940, just after the fall of France, there was a brief revival, when another generation of businessmen-volunteers, impatient at their country's laggard preparations, spent a month of basic military training at their own expense at the camp by the lake.) In a time of confusion the Plattsburg idea clarified the issues by visibly bringing home to America the idea of preparedness. It helped prod a reluctant President into a more active defense policy. In 1917, it did much in laying the groundwork for willing acceptance of the draft that had been so riotously resisted during another national crisis in 1863. Welcomed by most, dreaded by some, the Plattsburg idea was twentieth-century America's first tentative step toward universal military service.

In the late twenties, Francis Russell spent a summer at the Citizens' Military Training Camp at Fort Ethan Allen, Vermont; later he attended a Business Men's Training Camp at Fort Devens, Massachusetts. This article, along with several others that AMERICAN HERITAGE *has published, will appear as chapters in Mr. Russell's newest book,* The Great Interlude, *due this month from McGraw-Hill.*

For further reading: Leonard Wood, by Hermann Hagedorn (Harper, 1930).

LETTERS TO THE EDITORS

IN MEMORIAM, J.F.K.

In your December issue you enclosed a tribute to the late President Kennedy —a poem of Emily Dickinson's written in 1865. . . . Both my husband and myself feel that the eight-line poem expressed better how most of us felt than all the millions of words that were written about Mr. Kennedy's death.

Mrs. Harry Kronman
Santa Monica, California

At first I was astonished that The Magazine of History had chosen so personal an expression of grief as Emily Dickinson's poem. But I soon saw it was a perfect choice, for one of the most incredible features of this terrible and incredible business is that so many of us feel so personal a sorrow for a man we never laid eyes on.

Mrs. Cyril Sumner
Damariscotta, Maine

VICE VS. VIRTUE

I am writing to protest the insolence of the author of "Vice vs. Virtue, A Puritan Remembrancer," in the December, 1963, AMERICAN HERITAGE. The question is not ". . . how could . . . people, . . . many of them our own forebears, have taken such things so literally and seriously?" The issue is, how could people in only a few decades degenerate to the point of openly ridiculing truth and righteousness? . . . There are still people in America to whom some things are sacred and honorable.

Rev. J. Walter Jepson
Sacramento, California

WAS PREVOST IDLE?

War-of-1812 buffs hereabouts have greatly enjoyed Mr. C. S. Forester's excellent article on the Plattsburg campaign in the [December] issue of AMER-ICAN HERITAGE. But we think that the evidence contained in the enclosed selection from a British soldier's campaign diary may lead Mr. Forester to modify or withdraw his statement that, on the day of the attack on Plattsburg "Prevost stayed idle in his lines." [The anonymous diarist's entry for September 11, 1814, the date of the Battle of Plattsburg, reads in part: "In the morning our shipping were seen to be on the move. We then, that part of the army under Major Genl Robinsons command consisting of the 3d battn of the 27th regt and 76 regt and 4 light companies; and Major Genl Powers brigade consisting of the 3d 5th first battn of the 27th and 58th regts [began] to force the road to the Saranac and advance provided with scaling ladders to destroy the enemys works on the heights. . . . Scarcely had His Majestys troops . . . ascended the heights . . . when we heard the shout of victory from the enemys works in consiquence of the British flag being lowered on board the Confiance and Linnett and the gun boats seeking for safty in flight. Hear we found the enemy in the occupation of an ellavated ridge of land on the south side of the Saranac crowned with three strong redoubts and other field works and block houses armed with heavy ordinence. . . . This day we retreated a cross the Saranac again as our force was not strong enough."] This eye-witness account makes it clear that a land assault was launched as soon as the British naval squadron was seen to be moving into action and that it continued until Macdonough's victory was beyond doubt. Let me add that there are no apologists for Sir George Prevost in this camp!

E. C. Beer, Archivist
Queen's University
Kingston, Ontario

Mr. Forester replies:
I have said that "Prevost stayed idle in his lines" and I see no reason to modify this statement. A divisional general pushed a reconnaissance across the Saranac, presumably to make certain that the Americans were still in their lines; it cannot have been more than a reconnaissance when the casualty list totalled no more than thirty-seven. The two brigades mentioned must have numbered nearly 4,000 men, and any serious move could only have resulted in a loss ten times as great as was actually experienced.

WASHINGTON AT VALLEY FORGE

On page 101 of the Oct. '63 issue of AMERICAN HERITAGE you characterize as apocryphal the story of Washington praying in the woods at Valley Forge. Please inform me of reading matter that supports the view you present. I am inclined to agree with you, but I'd like to have some basis for asserting it to pupils.

M. K. Stone
Philadelphia, Pennsylvania

The best summation of the evidence is in George Washington and Religion, *by Paul F. Boller, Jr., (Southern Methodist University Press, 1963) pp. 8–11. Boller says that the Valley Forge story is "without foundation in fact," despite its being the favorite, perhaps, of all those who wish to make Washington a pious figure. Its inventor was the same Parson Weems who invented the story of Washington and the cherry tree.*

SNOBS AND TYRANTS

Your handsomely got-up October issue contains at least two articles in which the Republicans, as usual, come off as snobs, tyrants, inept little men. . . . Why not a nice little article about the character and habits of "Honey Fitz" Fitzgerald? Or Tammany Hall? . . .

Mrs. Arthur B. Loder
San Antonio, Texas

We published an article on Boston's Mayor James Curley ("The Last of the Bosses") in our June, 1959, issue. One on "Honey Fitz" was in fact scheduled for our last issue, but has been postponed for obvious reasons. A feature on Boss Tweed of Tammany Hall is coming soon.

The Trumpeter of Doomsday CONTINUED FROM PAGE 37

burg on September 11, 1814, declaring a few hours afterward: "I am satisfied that I can fight. I know I am no coward . . . Three of my men are wounded by a shell which burst within two feet of me."

In June of 1815, however, he emerged from the Army "completely disgusted with man's public character," and returned to farming, this time back at Low Hampton with his wife and little son. There he found existence "too monotonous . . . it appeared to me that there was nothing good on earth. Those things in which I had expected to find some solid good had deceived me. . . . The heavens were as brass over my head, and the earth as iron under my feet . . . I was truly wretched, but did not understand the cause."

Recent studies in the psychology of sudden religious conversion, such as Dr. William Sargant's *Battle for the Mind,* have thrown a great deal of light upon the characteristic tensions leading to Miller's own dramatic about-face and those of some of his later converts. His earlier devout upbringing had provided him with a constant concern for the future, accompanied by what he called tormenting doubts "respecting our condition in another state." Meanwhile, the silent reproaches of his wife and other pious relatives left him with feelings of guilt about his profane military language and infidel scoffings. While the works of Hume and Voltaire, Tom Paine and Ethan Allen had delighted his intellect, they had left his strong underlying emotional nature unsatisfied. In this state of undefined anxiety, Miller was ripe for that "escape from fear into love, from heaviness into joy" which a return to religion offered him.

The liberating vision came to him in 1816 at the little Baptist church of Low Hampton, whereupon he tells us, "the Scriptures became a delight . . . my mind became settled and satisfied." He soon became a pillar of the church, but his former deistic associates quickly challenged him to make good by logic his new conviction that the Bible contained none of the errors and contradictions which they found in it. Miller was now in the uncomfortable position of having to deny what he had stoutly affirmed, and to affirm what he had emphatically denied.

Consequently the Bible "became his chief study." He "lost all taste for other reading" in his desperate concentration on the crucial issue of man's immortality and future judgment. To this task he applied himself "with the most intense interest, whole nights as well as days being devoted to that object." His only aids were the marginal references and a concordance, which enabled him to "examine all the texts of Scripture in

which were found any of the prominent words contained in any obscure portion. Then by letting every word have its proper bearing on the subject of the text, if my view of it harmonized with every collateral passage in the Bible, it ceased to be a difficulty."

The first two years of this course of solitary reading and comparing convinced Miller that "the Bible is its own interpreter," and that although its prophecies were usually couched in figurative language, they were fulfilled literally, as the studies of secular historians testified. If the dates of minor catastrophes—the flood, the destruction of Pharaoh's hosts, and the wandering in the wilderness—had been predicted exactly, was it not reasonable to suppose that the date of the greatest cataclysm of all, the end of the world, was fixed somewhere in the Bible? The basis for Miller's rigid literalism was laid down in his fourteen "Rules of Interpretation," which declared that whenever all Bible texts on a subject were brought together "without a contradiction," then "the believer cannot be in error."

As for the Bible's figurative language, his Rule VIII stated that "Figures always have a figurative meaning, and are used much in prophecy, to represent future things, times and events, such as *mountains* meaning *governments, beasts* meaning *kingdoms, waters* meaning *people* . . . and *day* meaning *year.*"

Had Miller been asked how he knew exactly what each of these biblical expressions symbolized, he would have replied by giving one or more references in which, according to his interpretation, the context indicated that particular meaning. The fallacy is obvious, since a single or occasional use of a figure of speech does not make it, as he supposed, a fixed symbol. There may indeed be scriptural passages in which the word "day" is used to indicate a year or a century or a millennium. But it is absurd to conclude that it must always do so.

Armed with these "scientific" methods and his narrow, unscientific premises, Miller did not hesitate to tackle the knottiest of Bible passages, such as the mysterious outpourings of the prophet Daniel, King Nebuchadnezzar's dream, and the visions of the Apocalypse. In the words of his disciple and biographer, Sylvester Bliss: "At times puzzled and almost distracted by seemingly inexplicable or contradictory passages, he persevered until the application of his great principle of interpretation was triumphant." Despite the intricacy of his hypotheses, he believed that they formed, when rightly construed, a consistent system pointing to the destruction of this world and its wicked, unbelieving inhabitants at the Second Coming of Christ.

By 1818 he had become convinced that he had found the master key to unlock the prophetic chronology and reveal the precise date of the awesome event. It was the prophecy contained in Daniel 8:14: "Unto two thousand and three hundred days, then shall the sanctuary be cleansed." To the mind of William Miller, it was crystal clear that the "sanctuary" was the earth, long since desecrated, and that its "cleansing" was to be by fire at the return of the Messiah. Furthermore, this event was to take place in 2,300 "days," which he already had determined meant chronological years. The only remaining problem was: When had the "desolation of the holy place," the earth, begun? Miller held that the date was 457 B.C., when (according to Ezra 7:11–26) the commandment to rebuild Jerusalem was given. The rest was simple arithmetic: subtracting 457 from 2,300, he found that the world would come to an end in 1843 A.D. (Miller used the *ancient* Jewish calendar, so that the end of "1843" would come at the spring equinox, or March 21, 1844.)

There were four additional methods of calculating the Advent, all of which added up to exactly the same year: 1843. So Miller could hardly avoid, as a disciple wrote, the "solemn conclusion that in about 25 years from that time [1818], all the affairs of our present state would be wound up; that all its pride and power, pomp and vanity, wickedness and oppression, would come to an end; and that, in the place of the kingdoms of this world, the peaceful and long-desired kingdom of the Messiah would be established under the whole Heaven." The prospect filled Miller's heart with joy, but it did not impel him to rush out to warn the wicked of their impending doom. He wanted to be absolutely sure that his fearsome prophecy would not mislead anyone. The five years from 1818 to 1823 were to be spent in "weighing various objections" to his calculations; and then it was eight years more before he was ready to "go tell the world of the danger."

The first phase of his remarkable public career began with what he regarded as a providential call to lecture at a neighboring Baptist church. It came on a Sunday in August, 1831, with the prospect of "no preaching" that day at Dresden, New York, sixteen miles from where he lived. Would Miller fill the gap with a discourse on the Second Coming of Christ? He was understandably reluctant to go. He was fifty years old, aged beyond his years by an illness contracted in the Army, a layman without theological training. But inwardly he was bursting with the pent-up results of fourteen years of intensive study of prophecy, which had carried him into calculations almost as complex, in their own odd way, as those involved in the programming of a shot aimed at the moon.

So profound was Miller's effect upon his first listeners that he found himself with "a revival on his hands," and was urged to stay during the week and continue his lecturing. Invitations poured in thick and fast; he could not accept half of them. Yet in the first year of his "call" he delivered at least a hundred lectures, and he was to keep up this pace for many years despite ill health and limited funds.

Many conditions in the 1830's and 1840's favored the acceptance of Miller's disturbing doctrines by the rank and file of the rural fundamentalist churches and their ministers, in spite of the indifference and even the hostility of the more sophisticated urban clergy. In the country towns and villages, where evangelical Protestantism held sway, the Bible was still the virtually unchallenged authority; and the revivals led by Charles G. Finney and others had accustomed lethargic congregations to periodic "refreshings" of their religious zeal. (See "Pentecost in the Backwoods," by Bernard A. Weisberger, in the June, 1959, AMERICAN HERITAGE.) In addition, the panic of 1837 had stirred up widespread economic anxiety, and this was easily transformed into spiritual anxiety.

As the dread year of 1843 came nearer, public interest in the Millerite movement naturally became more intense. Not only was the number of believers growing rapidly, but there was a tendency to interpret various meteorological phenomena in ways that lent plausibility to Miller's claims. Northern lights, meteoric showers, and tornadoes seemed to take on increased significance; and in March of 1843 there happened to appear the most brilliant comet of the century, clearly visible even by daylight.

There were certain sober and logical steps which persons might have been expected to take who believed implicitly that the earth and their unbelieving neighbors were about to be destroyed, and themselves transported heavenward—abandoning one's business or property, forgiving one's creditors, and so on. One small boy in a Millerite household in Eastport, Maine, said to his mother quite sensibly that, as long as the world was about to end anyway, why not kill all the chickens and hens, and have a good feed before the time came?

But the public craves the picturesque, and the proceedings of the Millerites which attracted the most attention and excited the most ridicule were not rational preparations for the Advent, but the various "symbolic acts" induced among them by the prospect of coming deliverance. Here it is not always easy to separate legend from history, since hoaxers and scoffers were plentiful, and the press of the day was almost uniformly hostile. Impossible stories were told about "crazy Miller," who, as one editor acknowledged, "was probably the object of more abuse, ridicule, and blackguardism than any other man living."

Most widely celebrated and most vehemently disputed of all the symbolic acts associated with the movement was the alleged making and wearing of white ascension robes. The idea appealed so irresistibly to cartoonists and chroniclers that the legend will probably never be completely scotched by any number of documented denials—any more than it was by the indignant denials of Millerite leaders when the movement was at its height. It was undoubtedly in harmony with the popular image encouraged by scoffers, some of whom may themselves have dressed up in ascension robes in order to make fun of the faithful.

In like manner, the idea of "going up" generated the belief that many Millerites awaited the end in some elevated spot for greater ease in taking off, sometimes by climbing the nearest hill, or a tall tree, or the roof of a building. Many humorous stories were told of Millerites who, believing that the final moment had come, launched themselves into the air from such take-off points—only to descend, of course, ignominiously and with bruised buttocks. Another favorite story told of the misfortune of a local Millerite—the identity changed with the locale—who, forlornly returning home after the great disappointment, was refused entry by unconverted members of the family: they kept the door resolutely shut and called out, "Oh no, you can't be So-and-So. He [or she] has gone up."

It was said that some Millerites, instead of seeking elevated positions, preferred to wait for the end in

It was difficult to visualize the Second Coming, but artists never stopped trying. A typical conception is shown above.

graveyards, so as to join buried relatives or friends at the resurrection hour. Other groups were content merely to assemble in fields. One such "company of believers," more class-conscious than most, is described by Jane Marsh Parker, daughter of a Millerite preacher, thus:

They went out from Philadelphia some five miles near the Schuylkill along the Darby Road, pitching their tents in an open field, and gave themselves to prayer and praise while they awaited the sounding of the last trumpet. There were some highly-bred ladies among them—enthusiasts in the faith —and it was whispered at the time that a spirit of exclusiveness had dictated the withdrawal of the little company from the multitude of believers who assembled . . . in the public hall of the city; that even in such a democratic event as an ascension into the heavens it was the wish of certain old-family Philadelphians not to "go up" with the common crowd.

Common repute often attributed to the Millerites the symbolic acts indulged in by members of other radical religious sects as re-enactments of miscellaneous scriptural precedents. In Maine the Portland *Argus* stated that the Millerites of the town of Atkinson, in Piscataqua County, were

taking special pains to humble themselves, and for this purpose wash and kiss each other's feet—creep on the floor, etc. In some instances their conduct is revolting in the extreme. Take this case, which recently occurred—a pious, virtuous woman felt it her duty, as she stated, to appear before the assembly she was addressing entirely naked. This supposed duty she at once discharged by loosening her cloak and shawl —the only garments she had on—and letting them drop to the floor!

Undoubtedly dozens of these lurid tales were journalistic fabrications, based on rare instances which were quickly acknowledged and denounced by the leadership. "Certainly," says Francis D. Nichol, author of the apologetic book *The Midnight Cry*, "there were fanatical acts in connection with Millerism . . . it was troubled with fanatics."

In the early stages of his public appearances (his church did not license him to preach until late in 1833, and he was never ordained), Miller took great pains to avoid emotional excesses. But he underestimated the explosive impact of his solemn warnings upon the impressionable, ill-tutored, and even unbalanced minds in his audiences. And he did not foresee that the very success of his movement would take it out of his control and into the hands of men less scrupulous about using fear and fits in garnering recruits.

With all the favorable circumstances for the epidemic spread of Adventism in America of the 1830's, Miller's influence might have remained that of a typical rural revivalist had it not been for his encounter with the Reverend Joshua V. Himes, pastor of the

Chardon Street Baptist Chapel in Boston, in December, 1839. Himes, a restless agitator by nature, quickly embraced Miller's views, but declared that "the whole thing is kept in a corner yet," and proposed a number of ambitious plans "to diffuse it throughout the world." It has become customary to identify Himes as "the veritable Aaron to the Moses" of William Miller, but there are moments when the name of Barnum seems almost as appropriate. For Himes was a gifted and tireless publicist, and he lost no time in launching Millerism on the national market. His methods were professional. Two large newspapers were established, *The Signs of the Times* in Boston and *The Midnight Cry* in New York, while a steady stream of books and pamphlets issued from the presses. "Father Miller," as he had become known, was under increasing physical pressure ("I have more business on hand

Such phenomena as earthquakes and meteors were interpreted by Millerites as proving the imminence of the Advent.

than any two men like me should perform"), but his lectures to crowded congregations during this period were described, as usual, as "interspersed with powerful admonitions to the wicked; and he handles the Universalists with gloves of steel."

In the earlier, simpler days Miller and his apostles found many friendly pulpits, but as their popularity grew and the day of doom drew nearer, the established clergy began to take the offensive against them. Miller wrote to his eldest son from Philadelphia early in 1843: "Here, as in all other places, the D.D.s and priests, the clergy and editors, are out upon us with all their ribaldry and lies." The followers of the prophet, rather than Miller himself, began to think increasingly in terms of separate camp meetings and tents and tabernacles of their own. The ever-active Himes provided visual aids for the camp meetings in the form of big lithographs (see page 34), "upon one of

which," wrote the poet John G. Whittier, who visited the campground at East Kingston, New Hampshire, in the summer of 1842, "was the figure of a man, the head of gold, the breast and arms of silver, the belly of brass, the legs of iron, and the feet of clay,—the dream of Nebuchadnezzar. On the other were depicted the wonders of the apocalyptic vision—the beasts, the dragons, the scarlet woman seen by the seer of Patmos, Oriental types, figures, and mystic symbols, translated into staring Yankee realities, and exhibited like the beasts of a travelling menagerie. One horrible image with its hideous heads and scaly caudal extremity, reminded me of the tremendous line of Milton, who, in speaking of the same evil dragon, describes him as 'Swindging the scaly horrors of his folded tail.'"

At the East Kingston camp meeting $1,000 was raised to purchase a tent 120 feet in diameter, capable of holding 3,000 to 5,000 people, which was pitched eight times in cities all the way from Concord, New Hampshire to Newark, New Jersey, in the period from July to November, 1842. But promoter Himes was not satisfied. It was his idea to build on Howard Street in Boston a circular tabernacle, 115 feet in diameter, to seat 3,000 or more persons. It cost $4,000. Following its dedication on May 4, 1843, Himes held daily services there, with crowds whose singing could be heard for blocks; and sometimes equally large crowds of doubters would gather on Boston Common in the inconsistent hope of seeing the Millerites "go up." *

As the fateful year 1843 arrived, the tempo of Millerism accelerated, and it reached its widest propagation, extending from lower Canada to Virginia and Kentucky, as far west as Ohio and Michigan. Yet the greatest, most urgent, and most terrifying asset of the Millerite preachers, the limit of time before the final judgment day, might soon become their fatal liability. In the first issue of *The Midnight Cry*, Himes had declared that the movement "was not a distinct religious sect, but an *alarm*, and a CRY." Writing in 1842, Millerite G. F. Cox posed the question, "But what if 1843 should pass, and the event not arrive?" and answered, "The sentinel had better fire a false alarm, nay ten false alarms rather than suffer the enemy to approach, unexpected . . ." Miller himself, however, knew what the failure of his prophecy would mean: "If time continues until the end of this Jewish year [March 21, 1844] we shall be assailed by the enemy in every place where he can have any prospect of hurling in a dart."

To the consternation of the Adventists, time con-

* After the collapse of the movement, the tabernacle became the Howard Athenaeum, which burned down in February, 1846, to be replaced by Boston's long-time temple of the art of burlesque, the Old Howard, only recently razed.

tinued; and with jeers the darts were hurled. Miller had sometimes been scornful of ministers who differed with him, and some of them were quick to seize this opportunity to reciprocate. Six weeks after the last day of the prophetic year 1843—that is, in May, 1844—Miller issued a frank statement: *"I confess my error, and acknowledge my disappointment,* yet I still believe that the day of the Lord is near, even at the door . . ."
To a New York newspaper reporter the old man appeared bewildered: "One moment he would confess that he was mistaken, and the next day that he could discover no possible mistake, and go over his old calculations . . ." The Bible could not be wrong; the error must have been human, possibly due to the lapse of some secular historian.

But those who expected large numbers of Millerites to give up in dismay at this first disappointment greatly underestimated the resiliency of mind of the true believers. The crusade had attained enough momentum to keep the camp meetings going into August of 1844; and at one of them, in Exeter, New Hampshire, it was suggested that perhaps Miller had failed to notice that the commandment to rebuild Jerusalem was issued after the *seventh month* of the year 457 B.C., and that therefore the 2,300 years would terminate "on the tenth day of the seventh month" according to the sacred Jewish calendar, or on October 22, 1844.

The original fervor of those in attendance was immediately rekindled, and soon reached even greater heights than before. At the close of the meeting they took up the chant—from the New Testament parable of the wise and foolish virgins—*"Behold, the bridegroom cometh, go ye out to meet Him!"* At first this was only a movement within a movement, for the Millerite leaders dreaded, with reason, a second failure. Miller himself, a tired and ill old man, did not fully accept the new reckoning until about two weeks before the new "Last Great Day of Hope." Extra editions of Millerite papers then proclaimed the positively guaranteed date of climax. At the offices of *The Midnight Cry* in New York, "four steam presses were kept almost constantly in motion." Consistent to the last, the editors of the *Advent Herald* announced in their October 16 edition (given away free): "We shall make no provision for issuing a paper for the week following." Some farmers left their crops unharvested, shopkeepers closed their doors, and workers quit their jobs.

In spite of an increased amount of mob violence in the vicinity of the tabernacles, the solemn gatherings of the Millerites on the last day they expected to spend on earth seem to have been decorous enough, although there were scattered instances of erratic behavior. But the sun went down as usual on October 22, and nothing had happened. The tension grew unbearable as

midnight sounded—not on seraphic trumpets, but only on village clocks. The last stroke tolled. The great illusion was shattered.

"Our fondest hopes and expectations were blasted," wrote one Millerite leader afterward, "and such a spirit of weeping came over us as I never experienced before. . . . We wept, and wept, till the day dawn[ed] . . . I mused in my own heart. . . . If this had proved a failure, what was the rest of my Christian experience worth? Has the Bible proved a failure? Is there no God, no heaven, no golden home city, no paradise? Is all this but a cunningly devised fable?" Said another, a well-known Millerite lecturer: "The 22d of October passed, making unspeakably sad the faithful and longing ones; but causing the unbelieving and wicked to rejoice. All was still. No *Advent Herald;* no meetings. . . . Everyone felt lonely, with hardly a desire to speak to anyone. Still in the cold world!" And Josiah Litch, one of Miller's closest companions in the faith, wrote painfully to Miller on October 24: "It is a cloudy and dark day here—the sheep are scattered—and the Lord has not come yet."

At Low Hampton, Miller himself described October 22 as "a solemn time, when even the scoffers stood mute." Then, "it passed, and the next day it seemed

---

"Watch therefore, for ye know neither the day nor the hour wherein the Son of man cometh."
MATTHEW 25:13

---

as though all the demons from the bottomless pit were let loose upon us. The same ones and many more who were crying for mercy two days before, were now mixed with the rabble and mocking, scoffing, and threatening, in a most blasphemous manner." Yet before his death, on December 20, 1849, Miller managed to rally his confused and discordant believers at a "Mutual Conference of Adventists" in Albany, New York in April, 1845, which proved to be the seed bed from which the separate Adventist churches sprang—including, for example, Jehovah's Witnesses.

In the wake of the Second Advent fiasco the principal sufferers were the rural churches. This was not because most of the Millerites failed to resume their pews, but rather because of the damage done to the morale of all the evangelical communions. In 1846 the General Baptist Convention of Vermont declared: "The Second Advent delusion has proved the greatest calamity that has befallen us since our organization." The newspapers agreed: "There has been a long time of spiritual death and famine" (*Vermont Observer,* March, 1845); "an almost total dearth of revivals throughout the country, a moral chill has pervaded the churches, and a deathlike stupor on the minds of the impenitent, the like of which has not often been witnessed" (Poultney *Observer,* same month). All this increased the genuine distress of the old gentleman who had stirred up the turmoil and fanaticism.

For William Miller was no illiterate and superstitious exhorter solely concerned with terrifying his audiences into conversion, but a sober student of the Word, deeply convinced and deadly in earnest about what he believed he had found in it. Totally dedicated to his mission, at the same time that he supported a wife and eight children by farming, he spent over $2,000 of his own meager funds on his long tours of evangelism. What he did was to refurbish an ancient hope preached by American Protestant divines as far back as John Cotton's *The Pouring Out of the Seven Vials* in 1642. Most of his predecessors, and many of his contemporaries, were convinced that America was the predestined scene of Christ's return.

What Miller added to the traditional fire-and-brimstone mixture was the ingredient of mathematical computation as an "infallible" method of unravelling mysterious prophecies. This appealed strongly to Yankee ingenuity, and challenged the competitive spirit of thousands of amateur Bible-interpreters. In addition, he laid great stress upon the imminent casting down of the mighty, the wealthy, and the educated from their exalted seats, and the raising up of the weak and humble and faithful to replace them. More than that,

"And behold a fourth beast, dreadful and terrible, which was diverse from all the others and exceedingly dreadful."

in an age of competing utopias, when reformers were sprouting everywhere and promising everything—the "Madmen, Madwomen, Men with beards, Dunkers, Muggletonians, Come-Outers, Groaners, Agrarians, Seventh-Day Baptists, Quakers, Abolitionists, Calvinists, Unitarians, and Philosophers" listed by Emerson as attending the 1843 "Convention of Friends of Universal Reform"—Miller outbid them all.

For it was Miller who announced that with comparatively little constructive effort on man's part, except belief, he was about to be raised in one step, and in a measurable time, to that perfect society which the piecemeal reformers were promising would be his only after much time and effort. There need be no long preparatory campaigns for the achievement of the state of complete blessedness; all that was needed was the ingathering of the elect. To a substantial multitude Miller's appeal seemed indeed to be the long awaited midnight cry, to be heeded before it was too late— forever.

Harold A. Larrabee is Ichabod Spencer Professor of Philosophy, Emeritus, at Union College, Schenectady. One of his articles in AMERICAN HERITAGE, *"A Near Thing at Yorktown" (October, 1961), is to be published soon in expanded book form as* Decision at the Chesapeake *(Clarkson N. Potter).*

For further reading: Days of Delusion, *by Clara Endicott Sears (Houghton Mifflin, 1924);* Yankee Kingdom, *by Ralph Nading Hill (Harper, 1960).*

The Birth of Jim Crow

CONTINUED FROM PAGE 55

the Fourteenth Amendment. Citing numerous decisions of lower federal courts to the effect that accommodations did not have to be identical to be equal, the court as expected upheld the law.

"We have been at pains to expound this statute," added the court, "because the dissatisfaction felt with it by a portion of the people seems to us so unreasonable that we can account for it only on the ground of some misconception."

Chief Justice Francis Redding Tillou Nicholls, heading the court that handed down this decision in 1892, had signed the Jim Crow act as governor when it was passed in 1890. Previously he had served as the "Redeemer" governor who took over Louisiana from the carpetbaggers in 1877 and inaugurated a brief regime of conservative paternalism. In those days Nicholls had denounced race bigotry, appointed Negroes to office,

and attracted many of them to his party.

L. A. Martinet wrote Tourgée that Nicholls in those years had been "fair & just to colored men" and had, in fact, "secured a degree of protection to the colored people not enjoyed under Republican Governors." But in November, 1892, the wave of Populist rebellion among the white farmers was reaching its crest in the South, and Judge Nicholls' change of course typified the concessions to racism that conservatives of his class made in their efforts to forestall or divert the rebellion. Nonetheless, at a further hearing Nicholls granted Plessy's petition for a writ of error that permitted him to seek redress before the Supreme Court of the United States.

The brief that Albion Tourgée submitted to the Supreme Court in behalf of Plessy breathed a spirit of equalitarianism that was more in tune with his carpetbagger days than with the prevailing spirit of the mid-nineties.

At the very outset, he advanced an argument in behalf of his client that unconsciously illustrated the paradox that had from the start haunted the American attempt to reconcile strong color prejudice with deep equalitarian commitments.

Plessy, he contended, had been deprived of property without due process of law. The "property" in question was the "reputation of being white." It was "the most valuable sort of property, being the master-key that unlocks the golden door of opportunity." Intense race prejudice excluded any man suspected of having Negro blood "from the friendship and companionship of the white man," and therefore from the avenues to wealth, prestige, and opportunity. "Probably most white persons if given the choice," he held, "would prefer death to life in the United States as *colored persons.*"

Since Tourgée had proposed that a person who was "nearly white" be selected for the test case, it may be presumed that he did so with this argument in mind. But this was not a defense of the colored man against discrimination by whites, but a defense of the "nearly" white man against the penalties of color. The argument, whatever its merits, apparently did not impress the Court.

Tourgée went on to develop more relevant points. He emphasized especially the incompatibility of the segregation law with the spirit and intent of the Thirteenth and particularly the Fourteenth amendments. Segregation perpetuated distinctions "of a servile character, coincident with the institution of slavery." He held that "slavery was a caste, a legal condition of subjection to the dominant class, a bondage quite separable from the incident of ownership." He scorned the pretense of impartiality and equal protection advanced in the defense of the "separate but equal" doctrine.

"The object of such a law," he declared, "is simply to debase and distinguish against the inferior race. Its purpose has been properly interpreted by the general designation of 'Jim Crow Car' law. Its object is to separate the Negroes from the whites in public conveyances for the gratification and recognition of the sentiment of white superiority and white supremacy of right and power." He asked the members of the Court to imagine the tables turned and themselves ordered into a Jim Crow car. "What humiliation, what rage would then fill the judicial mind!" he exclaimed.

The clue to the true intent of the Louisiana statute was that it did not apply "to nurses attending the children of the other race." On this clause Tourgée shrewdly observed:

The exemption of nurses shows that the real evil lies not in the color of the skin but in the relation the colored person sustains to the white. If he is a dependent it may be endured: if he is not, his presence is insufferable. Instead of being intended to promote the *general* comfort and moral well-being, this act is plainly and evidently intended to promote the happiness of one class by asserting its supremacy and the inferiority of another class. Justice is pictured blind and her daughter, the Law, ought at least to be color-blind.

Tourgée then asked the Court to look to the future. Should the separate-car law be upheld, he inquired, "what is to prevent the application of the same principle to other relations?" Was there any limit to such laws? "Why not require all colored people to walk on one side of the street and whites on the other? . . . One side of the street may be just as good as the other. . . . The question is not as to the *equality* of the privileges enjoyed, but *the right of the State to label one citizen as white and another as colored* in the common enjoyment of a public highway."

The Supreme Court did not get around to handing down a decision on *Plessy v. Ferguson* until 1896. In the years that intervened between the passage of the Louisiana segregation law in July, 1890, and the time of the eventual decision on its constitutionality in 1896, the retreat from the commitment to equality had quickened its pace in the South and met with additional acquiescence, encouragement, and approval in the North. Two states had already disfranchised the Negro, and several others, including Louisiana, were planning to take the same course. In 1892 Congress defeated the Lodge Bill, designed to extend federal protection to elections, and in 1894 it wiped from the federal statute books a mass of Reconstruction laws for the protection of equal rights. And then, on September 18, 1895, Booker T. Washington delivered a famous speech embodying the so-called "Atlanta Compromise," which was widely interpreted as an acceptance of subordinate status for the Negro by the foremost leader of the race.

On May 18, 1896, Justice Henry Billings Brown, a resident of Michigan but a native of Massachusetts, delivered the opinion of the Court in the case of *Plessy v. Ferguson*. His views upholding the defendant's case —that the "separate but equal" doctrine was constitutional—were in accord with those of all his brothers, with the possible exception of Justice David Josiah Brewer, who did not participate, and the certain exception of Justice John Marshall Harlan, who vigorously dissented in phrases that often echoed Tourgée's arguments. In approving, to all intents and purposes, the principle of segregation, Justice Brown followed not only the trend of the times, but a host of state judicial precedents, which he cited at length. That there were no federal judicial precedents to the contrary only added to the technical strength of his position. Just as telling, perhaps, was Brown's mention of the action of Congress in establishing segregated schools for the District of Columbia, an action endorsed by Radical Republicans who had supported the Fourteenth Amendment, and sustained in regular congressional appropriations ever since.

Similar laws, wrote Brown, were adopted by "the legislatures of many states, and have been generally, if not uniformly, sustained by the courts." The validity of such segregation laws, he maintained, depended on their "reasonableness." And in determining reasonableness, the legislature "is at liberty to act with reference to the established usages, customs, and traditions of the people, and with a view to the promotion of their comfort, and the preservation of the public peace and good order."

In addition to judicial precedent and accepted practice, Justice Brown ventured into the more uncertain fields of sociology and psychology for support of his opinion. He wrote:

We consider the underlying fallacy of the plaintiff's argument to consist in the assumption that the enforced separation of the two races stamps the colored race with a badge of inferiority. If this be so, it is not by reason of anything found in the act, but solely because the colored race chooses to put that construction upon it. . . . The argument also assumes that social prejudices may be overcome by legislation, and that equal rights cannot be secured by the negro except by an enforced commingling of the two races. We cannot accept this proposition. . . . Legislation is powerless to eradicate racial instincts, or to abolish distinctions based upon physical differences, and the attempt to do so can only result in accentuating the difficulties of the present situation. If the civil and political rights of both races be equal, one cannot be inferior to the other civilly or politically. If one race be inferior to the other socially, the constitution of the United States cannot put them upon the same plane.

One of the most fascinating paradoxes in American jurisprudence is that the opinion of a native son of Massachusetts, Brown, should have bridged the gap between the radical equalitarian commitment of 1868 and the reactionary repudiation of that commitment in 1896; and that Harlan, a southerner, should have bridged the greater gap between the repudiation of 1896 and the radical rededication to the equalitarian idealism of 1868 in 1954. For the dissenting opinion of Justice Harlan, embodying many of the arguments of Plessy's ex-carpetbagger counsel, foreshadowed the Court's eventual repudiation of the *Plessy v. Ferguson* decision and the doctrine of "separate but equal" more than half a century later—a repudiation in which, fit-

tingly enough, Harlan's grandson and namesake on the Warren Court wholly concurred.

The elder John Marshall Harlan is correctly described by Robert Cushman as "a Southern gentleman and a slave-holder, and at heart a conservative." A Kentuckian of the Whig persuasion, Harlan had opposed secession and fought in the Union Army, but at the same time he opposed both the emancipation of the slaves and the passage of civil rights laws to protect the rights of the freedmen. Shocked by Ku Klux excesses, he experienced a sudden conversion, renounced his former views, became a Republican in 1868, and was appointed to the Supreme Court by President Hayes in 1877.

After his conversion Harlan became one of the most outspoken champions of Negro rights of his time, and during his thirty-four years on the bench he lifted his voice repeatedly against denial of those rights by the dominant opinion of the Court. His famous dissent in the Civil Rights Cases of 1883 had denounced the "subtle and ingenious verbal criticism" by which "the substance and spirit of the recent amendments of the Constitution have been sacrificed." And in 1896 he was ready to strike another blow for his adopted cause.

Harlan held the Louisiana segregation law in clear conflict with both the Thirteenth and the Fourteenth amendments. The former "not only struck down the institution of slavery," but also "any burdens or disabilities that constitute badges of slavery or servitude," and segregation was just such a burden or badge. Moreover, the Fourteenth Amendment "added greatly to the dignity and glory of American citizenship, and to the security of personal liberty," and segregation denied to Negroes the equal protection of both dignity and liberty. "The arbitrary separation of citizens, on the basis of race, while they are on a public highway," he said, "is a badge of servitude wholly inconsistent with the civil freedom and the equality before the law established by the constitution. It cannot be justified upon any legal grounds."

Harlan was as scornful as Tourgée had been of the claim that the separate-car law did not discriminate against the Negro. "Every one knows," he declared, that its purpose was "to exclude colored people from coaches occupied by or assigned to white persons." This was simply a poorly disguised means of asserting the supremacy of one class of citizens over another. The Justice continued:

But in view of the constitution, in the eye of the law, there is in this country no superior, dominant, ruling class of citizens. There is no caste here. Our constitution is color-blind, and neither knows nor tolerates classes among citizens. In respect of civil rights, all citizens are equal before the law. The humblest is the peer of the most powerful. The law regards man as man, and takes no account of his surroundings, or of his color when his civil rights as guaranteed by the supreme law of the land are involved. . . . We boast of the freedom enjoyed by our people above all other peoples. But it is difficult to reconcile that boast with a state of law which, practically, puts the brand of servitude and degradation upon a large class of our fellow citizens,—our equals before the law. The thin disguise of "equal" accommodations for passengers in railroad coaches will not mislead any one, nor atone for the wrong this day done.

"The present decision, it may well be apprehended," predicted Harlan, "will not only stimulate aggressions, more or less brutal and irritating, upon the admitted rights of colored citizens, but will encourage the belief that it is possible, by means of state enactments, to defeat the beneficent purposes which the people of the United States had in view when they adopted the recent amendments of the constitution. . . ." For if the state may so regulate the railroads, "why may it not so regulate the use of the streets of its cities and towns as to compel white citizens to keep on one side of a street, and black citizens to keep on the other," or, for that matter, apply the same regulations to streetcars and other vehicles, or to courtroom, the jury box, the legislative hall, or to any other place of public assembly?

"In my opinion," the Kentuckian concluded, "the judgment this day rendered will, in time, prove to be quite as pernicious as the decision made by this tribunal in the Dred Scott Case."

But Harlan was without allies on the Court, and the country as a whole received the news of its momentous decision upholding the "separate but equal" doctrine in relative silence and apparent indifference. Thirteen years earlier the Civil Rights Cases had precipitated pages of news reports, hundreds of editorials, indignant rallies, congressional bills, a Senate report, and much general debate. In striking contrast, the *Plessy* decision was accorded only short, inconspicuous news reports and virtually no editorial comment outside the Negro press. A great change had taken place, and the Court evidently now gave voice to the dominant mood of the country. Justice Harlan had spoken for the forgotten convictions of a bygone era.

The racial aggressions he foresaw came in a flood after the decision of 1896. Even Harlan indicated by his opinion of 1899 in *Cummings v. Board of Education* that he saw nothing unconstitutional in segregated public schools. Virginia was the last state in the South to adopt the separate-car law, and she resisted it only until 1900. Up to that year this was the only law of the type adopted by a majority of the southern states. But on January 12, 1900, the editor of the Richmond *Times* was in full accord with the new spirit

when he asserted: "It is necessary that this principle be applied in every relation of Southern life. God Almighty drew the color line and it cannot be obliterated. The negro must stay on his side of the line and the white man must stay on his side, and the sooner both races recognize this fact and accept it, the better it will be for both."

With a thoroughness approaching the incredible, the color line *was* drawn and the Jim Crow principle was applied even in those areas that Tourgée and Harlan had suggested a few years before as absurd extremes. In sustaining all these new laws, courts universally and confidently cited *Plessy v. Ferguson* as their authority. They continued to do so for more than half a century.

On April 4, 1950, Justice Robert H. Jackson wrote old friends in Jamestown, New York, of his surprise in running across the name of Albion W. Tourgée, once a resident of the nearby village of Mayville, in connection with segregation decisions then pending before the Supreme Court. "The *Plessy* case arose in Louisiana," he wrote, "and how Tourgée got into it I have not learned. In any event, I have gone to his old brief, filed here, and there is no argument made today that he would not make to the Court. He says, 'Justice is pictured blind and her daughter, the Law, ought at least to be color-blind.' Whether this was original with him, it has been gotten off a number of times since as original wit. Tourgée's brief was filed April 6, 1896 and now, just fifty-four years after, the question is again being argued whether his position will be adopted and what was a defeat for him in '96 be a postmortem victory."

Plessy v. Ferguson remained the law of the land for fifty-eight years lacking one day, from May 18, 1896, to May 17, 1954, when the Supreme Court at last renounced it in the school segregation cases of *Brown et al. v. Board of Education of Topeka*, et al. In that decision could indeed be found, at long last, a vindication, "a post-mortem victory"—not only for the ex-carpetbagger Tourgée, but for the ex-slaveholder Harlan as well.

Arkansas-born C. Vann Woodward, Sterling Professor of History at Yale, is the author of The Burden of Southern History *and of* Origins of the New South, *which won the Bancroft prize. His* The Strange Career of Jim Crow, *published by the Oxford University Press in 1955 (and subsequently in Oxford's paperback Galaxy series), is an excellent study of the history of segregation. Professor Woodward expresses indebtedness to Professor Paul A. Freund of the Harvard Law School for the letter of Justice Robert H. Jackson, and to Professor Otto Olsen of Old Dominion College at Norfolk for information about Albion W. Tourgée.*

with them, going to their meetings, protesting the increasing arrests, and writing religious tracts. He had not yet found his way of writing. *Truth Exalted* (1668), his first tract, was verbose and filled with the current exhortations. Another shaft, groaning under the title of *The Guide Mistaken and Temporizing Rebuked,* shortly followed. For writing *The Sandy Foundation Shaken,* in which he attacked the Trinity, Penn was arrested by the Privy Council on December 12, 1668, charged with failure to obtain a publishing license from the Bishop of London, and, as mentioned above, committed to the Tower for safe custody. John Evelyn was shocked and noted that "one of Sir William Pen's sons had published a blasphemous book against the Deity of our blessed Lord." But Pepys, who got his wife to read him Penn's book, found it "so well writ as, I think, it is too good for him ever to have writ it," and "a serious sort of book, and not fit for every body to read."

The warrant was issued by the Privy Council to Sir John Robinson, the Lord Lieutenant of the Tower, who would be Penn's prosecutor in the notorious trial two years later. The Bishop of London sent word to Penn that he could recant in Covent Garden at an appropriate time before the "Fair" of all the city or else be kept in prison for the rest of his life. Penn would not budge a jot; he said he owed his conscience to no mortal man; he had no need to fear; he valued not such threats. The King sent his chaplain, the Bishop of Worcester, to see him; the prospective life prisoner told Worcester that the Tower was the worst argument in the world to convince him. He also explained to the Bishop that he had not meant to deny the divinity of Christ, and agreed to write another pamphlet, clarifying his views. *Innocency With Her Open Face, Presented by Way of Apology for the Book Entitled, The Sandy Foundation Shaken,* was the result. In it Penn expounded his belief in Jesus Christ, despite his attack on the Trinity.

What could one do with a man like that? If you clapped him in the Tower he had time for his scandalous (and highly popular) attacks on the church, which were smuggled out of prison and sold everywhere—yet there was no doubt that he was a devout believer. If you let him out, at least he was more occupied with meetings and preachments, which were easier (perhaps) to handle. Besides, his father was a friend of the King, although the Admiral had recently been impeached and tried for embezzling prize goods (he was not convicted); and the King still owed the Admiral some sixteen thousand pounds.

Whatever the reason, William Penn was discharged from the Tower on July 28, 1669.

Three weeks after his release his father, still hoping he could get the young man away from this crusading which got one nowhere, sent him to Ireland to transact some business affairs; perhaps the trip would divert his mind from such unbecoming missionary zeal. But even while attending to his father's business in such improbable places as Imokilly and Shanagarry, Penn spent a good part of his year in Ireland engaged in strenuous efforts to relieve the persecution of Irish Quakers. Having achieved much success in both ventures, he returned to London in August, 1670. The famous "tryal" was but a few days off.

During that year the persecution of both Quakers and Catholics was renewed. Laws were amended to provide more speedy remedies against these "dangerous practices of seditious sectaries," and particularly the assemblies. In order to test the law, George Fox, the founder of the Quakers and a dedicated expert in rousing popular emotion, went to the Friends Meeting House in Gracechurch Street, where he expected the storm was most likely to begin. A large crowd had gathered to see what would happen to the Quakers. A file of musketeers appeared. Fox and two others were dragged away, and someone shouted: "Have a care of him, he is a princely man!" Public opinion was turning against the excesses of the government. Moved by Fox's eloquence, the mayor, Sir Samuel Starling, the same official who would soon try to convict Penn under like circumstances, dismissed the charge. Later George Whitehead returned to the same spot, where some Friends were listening to a Catholic priest. After the sermon Whitehead preached peace and love, was committed to prison, and fined twenty pounds. The meeting place of the Quakers was boarded up and many of them sent to jail. Like Mahatma Gandhi, like Martin Luther King, like all men who will not fight but also will not yield, these quiet Quakers were a dangerous lot, particularly when they had leaders like Fox and Penn.

Penn's next opportunity to be tested and proven worthy of his God came on August 14. He was preaching outdoors in Gracechurch Street before the closed meetinghouse, with Friend William Mead acting as a kind of assistant. A crowd of a few hundred people had assembled, expecting trouble, but there had been no violence, certainly none until the sheriff and soldiers arrived. The speaker was arrested under a writ signed by the Lord Mayor, directing the sheriff to receive under his custody the body of William Penn, taken for preaching seditiously and causing a tumult of the people. Instead of being brought to the foul depths of Newgate, Penn, being a gentleman, was lodged at the Black Dog at Newgate Market, where one could buy comfort. The next day he wrote his father that he had told the Mayor he could bear harsh expressions about himself but not about his father; the Mayor had said that the Admiral had starved his seamen. "Be not displeased or grieved," the son

continued. "What if this be designed of the Lord for an exercise of our patience?" Reading this, his father may have reflected how much and how often his own patience had been exercised by his son. "I am very well," the letter ended, "and have no trouble upon my spirits, besides my absence from thee." His heart seemed always to be light under adversity.

Two weeks later, on September 1, 1670, the trial against William Penn, gentleman, and William Mead, linen draper, began. The indictment was read. It charged the defendants and other unknown persons with assembling and congregating together to the "disturbance of the peace of the said Lord the King"; and recited that the defendant Penn by abetment with Mead did preach and speak, by reason whereof there followed "a great Concourse and Tumult of People," which remained and continued a long time in contempt of the King and his law "to the great disturbance of his Peace; to the great Terror and Disturbance of many of his Liege People and Subjects, to the ill Example of all others . . ."

"What say you, William Penn and William Mead, are you guilty or . . . not guilty?"

Penn demanded a copy of the indictment—how could he remember it verbatim?

The Recorder, presiding, answered that he must first plead.

Penn, assured that no advantage would be taken of him, pleaded "not guilty." The court very soon adjourned until the afternoon; and the anonymous "observer" to whom we are indebted for a lively account of the trial, and who was obviously outraged by the treatment that the prisoners received, suggests that it was the constant and unkind practice of the court to make prisoners "wait on the trials of Felons and Murderers, thereby designing in all probability, both to affront and tire them." When the adjournment ended late in the afternoon, there was an alter-

cation. The defendants were wearing their hats in court, having put them on when the Mayor asked who had ordered them off; now the court began to bait the prisoners—did they know the respect one showed to the court? If they did not pull off their hats they would be fined forty marks (about seventy-five dollars) apiece.

Penn now began his line of studied, polite insolence to the court, an attitude that lasted throughout the trial. He had tangled with Sir Samuel Starling before, and knew him for a man who stood on nothing but his dignity; and he quickly sized up the pompous Recorder as a bird of the same feather. The bench, said Penn, and not the defendants should be fined, since the bench had ordered the hats put on. Mead, backing up Penn's line a little cumbrously, called on all people to take notice of this injustice; and added, like some Greek chorus: "O fear the Lord, and dread his Power, and yield unto the Guidance of his Holy Spirit, for He is not far from every one of you."

Penn and Mead conducted their own case, without lawyers. The trial was in the Elizabethan manner, each side criticizing and contradicting the other, and speaking out of turn. Meanwhile the packed audience was applauding Penn, so that it had to be cautioned by the crier to keep silence upon pain of imprisonment.

Witnesses for the prosecution estimated the "great concourse" which the defendants had addressed at something between 300 and 500. The Recorder asked Mead what he thought the number was—had he been there? Mead quoted legal Latin back at him—"No man is bound to accuse himself . . . Why dost thou offer to ensnare me with such a question? . . . Doth not this show thy malice? Is this like unto a Judge that ought to be Counsel for the Prisoner at the Bar?"

The Recorder: "Sir, hold your tongue, I do not go about to ensnare you."

The room was in an uproar, and Penn suggested

that silence be demanded; and when this was done he briefly stated their case: They would not recant; they declined even to vindicate "the assembling of ourselves to preach, pray, or worship the Eternal, Holy, Just God . . ." It was "our indispensable duty to meet incessantly upon so good an account; nor shall all the powers upon Earth be able to divert us from reverencing and adoring our God who made us."

Alderman Brown interrupted to point out that Penn was not on trial for worshipping God, but for breaking the law.

Penn instantly affirmed that he had broken no law; and to the end that the bench, the jury, and himself, *"with those that hear us,"* might have a more direct understanding of the procedure, he desired to know by what law it was that he was prosecuted.

The Recorder, wary of a trap, answered "the Common Law"; and added, conscious that his reply sounded a little vague, that he could not be expected to "run up so many years, and over so many adjudged cases which we call Common Law," to answer Penn's curiosity.

Penn retorted that the answer was very short of his question; "if it be common, it should not be so hard to produce."

THE RECORDER (losing his temper): You are a saucy fellow, speak to the Indictment.

PENN: You are many mouths and ears against me . . . I say again, unless you show me *and the People* the law you ground your indictment upon [emphasis supplied—Penn never forgot his audience], I shall take it for granted your proceedings are merely arbitrary.

THE RECORDER (feeling himself cornered): The question is whether you are guilty of this indictment.

PENN: The question is not whether I am guilty of this indictment but whether this indictment be legal. . . . Where there is no law there is no transgression.

THE RECORDER (unable to answer this): You are an impertinent fellow. It's *lex non scripta* [law that is not written], that which many have studied thirty or forty years to know, and would you have me tell you in a moment?

Penn quoted the *Institutes* of Lord Coke (1552–1634), that implacable adherent of common law, referred to the privileges in Magna Charta, and cited statutes.

THE RECORDER (now thoroughly confused): Sir, you are a troublesome fellow, and it is not for the honour of the Court to suffer you to go on.

PENN: I have asked but one question, and you have not answered me; [then, doubtless, turning to the jury] though the rights and privileges of every Englishman be concerned in it.

THE RECORDER (his back against the wall): Sir, we must not stand to hear you talk all night.

PENN: If you deny me *oyer* [to be heard] of that law,

which you suggest I have broken, you do at once deny me an acknowledged right, and evidence to the whole World your resolution to sacrifice the privileges of Englishmen to your sinister and arbitrary views.

This was too much, and the Recorder, at the end of his rope, turned to the Mayor, crying: "Take him away. My Lord, if you take not some course with this pestilent Fellow, to stop his mouth, we shall not be able to do anything tonight."

The Mayor exclaimed, "Take him away, take him away, turn him into the bail-dock." (The bail-dock was a small room partitioned off in the corner of the courtroom.) Then Penn let himself go in grandiloquent speech to the jury: Was this justice? Must he be taken away because he pleaded the fundamental law of England? He left it to the conscience of the jury (his sole judge) that if these fundamental laws, which relate to liberty and property, be not maintained, "our liberties are to be openly invaded, our wives ravished, our children slaved, our families ruined, our estates led away in triumph by every sturdy beggar and malicious informer as their trophies . . . The Lord of Heaven and Earth will be judge between us in this matter." The word "informer" was a red rag to the crowd, who may have hissed when they heard it.

Penn was dragged to the bail-dock and Mead tried his hand at badgering their lordships, speaking directly to the jury: "You men of the jury, here I do now stand, to answer to an indictment against me, which is a Bundle of stuff, full of lies and falsehoods." He was accused of meeting illegally with force and arms. "Time was," he continued, "when I had freedom to use a carnal weapon, and then I thought I feared no

man; but now I fear the living God, and dare not make use thereof, nor hurt any man; nor do I know I demeaned myself as a tumultuous person . . . You men of the jury, who are my Judges, if the Recorder will not tell you what makes a riot, a rout, or an unlawful assembly—a riot is when three or more are met together to beat a man, or to enter forcibly into another man's land, to cut down his grass, his wood, or break down his poles . . ."

At this point the Recorder interrupted Mead, and said, pulling off his hat (a gesture he must have conceived to be biting sarcasm): "I thank you, Sir, that you will tell me what the law is."

To which Mead answered, disdainfully: "Thou may'est put on thy hat. I have never a fee for thee now."

Alderman Brown remarked that Mead talked at random, sometimes as an Independent, now as a Quaker, next as a Papist.

Mead answered impertinently in Latin, to the effect that the Alderman did not know what he was talking about.

THE MAYOR (losing his temper): You deserve to have your tongue cut out.

THE RECORDER: If you discourse in this manner, I shall take occasion against you.

MEAD: I am an Englishman, and you might be ashamed of this dealing.

RECORDER: I look upon you to be an enemy of the laws of England, which ought to be observed and kept, nor are you worthy of such privileges as others have.

MEAD: The Lord judge between me and thee in this matter.

That was again too much for the Recorder; and Mead also was placed in the bail-dock. In the absence of both defendants the Recorder charged the jury. Penn shouted his objection from the bail-dock "in a very raised voice," appealing to the jury, "who are my judges, and this great assembly." Were "the proceedings of the Court not most arbitrary, and void of all law in offering to give the jury their charge in the absence of the prisoners?" Again, citing chapter and verse from Coke, and from Magna Charta, he cried that he was thoroughly prepared to argue his own case. Whereupon the Recorder "being thus unexpectedly lashed for his extrajudicial procedure," said with a smug smile (according to the observer), "Why ye are present, ye do hear, do you not?"

"No thanks to the Court," Penn shouted; and continued: "You of the Jury take notice that I have not been heard." He had still at least ten or twelve material points to offer, he bellowed; and Mead added his objections to these "barbarous and unjust proceedings." The Recorder ordered them taken to the "hole,"

a sort of detention place in the Old Bailey, suggesting that it would not be to the honor of the court to hear them talk all night, "as they would."

The observer tells us that the jurors were commanded to agree upon their verdict, while the prisoners remained in the "stinking hole." After an hour and a half eight jurors came down, agreed on a verdict, and the court sent an officer to bring down the other four, who would not agree. They were Edward Bushell, John Hammond, Charles Milson, and John Baily. Edward Bushell was known to be their leader, and "the Bench [says the observer] used many unworthy threats on the four that dissented." The Recorder told Bushell that he was the cause of this "disturbance"; and added, "I shall set a mark [a fine] upon you, Sir." The prosecutor, Sir John Robinson, announced that he had known Bushell for fourteen years, and that he had thrust himself upon the jury: "I tell you, you deserve to be indicted more than any man that hath been brought to the Bar this day."

Bushell answered that he would willingly have avoided jury service, but had not been able to. Alderman Bludworth retorted that when he saw Mr. Bushell he knew that he would never yield: "Mr. Bushell, we know what you are." And the Mayor added: "Sirrah, you are an impudent fellow. I will put a mark upon you." According to the observer, the court used much menacing language, and behaved themselves imperiously toward the jury—all this because the four had refused to find Penn and Mead guilty. After this "barbarous language," the court sent the jurors out to reconsider the verdict.

After a considerable time the jury came back, stubborn as ever.

CLERK: Are you agreed in your verdict?

JURY: Yes.

CLERK: Who shall speak for you?

JURY: Our foreman.

CLERK: Look upon the prisoners at the Bar: Is William Penn Guilty of the matter whereof he stands indicted, in manner and form, or Not Guilty?

THE FOREMAN [Thomas Veer]: Guilty of speaking in Gracechurch Street.

THE COURT: *Is that all?*

THE FOREMAN: That is all I had in commission.

THE RECORDER: You had as good say nothing.

MAYOR: Was it not an Unlawful Assembly? You mean he was speaking to a tumult of people there?

FOREMAN (seeing the trap): My Lord, this is all I had in commission.

At this point, according to the observer, some of the jury seemed to "buckle" under the questions of the court, but the others would allow no such words as "unlawful assembly"; and the Recorder, the Mayor, the prosecutor, and Alderman Bludworth vilified them "with most opprobrious language." Finally the Mayor told them they had given no verdict, and that they should go and consider it again, so that an end might be made of this "troublesome business."

The jury had won the first two rounds, and Bushell must have harangued them during the half hour they were out. Their third verdict, signed by all twelve, was as queer, and as little satisfactory to the court, as the first. They found that William Penn was guilty of speaking or preaching to an assembly met together in Gracechurch Street on the fourteenth of August last, 1670. Obviously this was no "proper" verdict.

"This," says the observer, "the Mayor and Recorder resented at so high a rate, that they exceeded the bounds of all reason and civility." The Mayor asked them if they would be "led by such a silly fellow as Bushell." Then, addressing himself to the foreman: "I thought you had understood your place better"—meaning his duty to obey the court, and convict.

The court, the prisoners, the jury, and particularly the people knew what was at stake. The government was determined to stop forbidden religious assemblies, to break the spreading Quaker movement, and to use an instrument of the people, the jury, for such purposes. The Recorder said as much, frankly: "Gentlemen, you shall not be dismist till we have a Verdict that the Court will accept: and you shall be locked up without Meat, Drink, Fire, or tobacco; you shall not think thus to abuse the court; we will have a verdict, by the help of God, or you shall starve for it."

Penn, out of the bail-dock and back in court, objected: "The arbitrary resolves of the Bench may not be made the measure of my Jury's Verdict." The Recorder, again losing his temper, sputtered: "Stop that prating fellow's mouth, or put him out of the Court!"

As the court broke up, Penn continued to argue. The Quakers had made no tumult, as the Mayor claimed. Two soldiers with force and arms had closed the Friends' lawful meeting place. Now a verdict had been given, and Penn demanded, "I require the Clerk of the Court to record it, as he will answer it at his peril. And if the Jury bring in another Verdict contrary to this, I affirm they are perjured men in law."

As he was dragged out, Penn again appealed to the jury: "You are Englishmen, mind your privilege, give not away Your Right!" And Veer shouted back: "Nor will we ever do it." The jurors were sent out to spend the night without meat, drink, fire, or any other accommodation; and "they had not even so much as a chamber pot, tho' desired," as the observer sympathetically notes. The court adjourned to the next day, the fourth of the month at seven in the morning,

at which time the jury, as before, reported their finding—*guilty of speaking in Gracechurch Street*. Once more there were passages between jury and Mayor.

The jury, having received a fresh charge from the bench "to extort an unjust Verdict" (according to the observer), went up again, and for the third time the same colloquy took place on their return. Again the Recorder threatened Bushell: "You are a factious fellow, I will set a mark upon you; and whilst I have anything to do in the City, I will have an eye upon you"; and the Mayor, exasperated, lashed the others: "Have you no more wit than to be led by such a pitiful fellow? I will cut his nose!"

Here was another opening for Penn to pour out his angry eloquence. It was intolerable, he protested, that his jury should be thus menaced. Were these men not his judges under the Great Charter of England? What hope was there of ever having proper justice done when verdicts were rejected and juries were threatened with fines, starvation, and ruin to make them reach decisions contrary to their consciences?

In answer the Mayor, obviously hot and frightened as the faces of the crowd pressed against him, his self-control gone, could only cry out: "Stop his mouth, jailor, bring fetters and stake him to the ground!" The Recorder equally betrayed himself: "Till now I never understood the reason of the policy and prudence of the Spaniards, in suffering the Inquisition among them; and certainly it will never be well with us till something like the Spanish Inquisition be in England!"

This suggestion of the use of torture was no idle threat. Although torture was unknown in common law, it had been resorted to in England for several centuries as a means of obtaining evidence and for punishment. Torture could still be ordered by the Crown, the Privy Council, or by the Star Chamber, which was not bound by common law. *Peine forte et dure* might be used when the prisoner would not plead. He was "to be stretched upon his back, to have hot iron laid upon him as much as he could bear, and more, and so to continue, fed upon bad bread and stagnant water through alternate days until he pleaded or died." An instance of *peine* occurred as late as 1726, and was said to be common practice at the Old Bailey up to the eighteenth century.

The substance of this practice was doubtless known to Penn's jury. Half starved but wholly obstinate, they had not yet been broken. Being required to meet again to find another verdict, the observer says, they steadily refused. The Recorder, in great passion, was running off the bench, saying he would sit no longer to hear these things, when the Mayor made him stay, and told the jury to draw up another verdict that they might "bring it in special." The jury refused—they had set their hands to the verdict, they ought not to be returned to the hole. But the sheriffs were ordered to take the jury up again and sworn to keep them without any accommodation till they brought in their verdict; and the Recorder again threatened them: they should starve until a proper verdict was brought in; "I will have you carted about the city as in Edward the Third's time."

They returned once more from Newgate at seven the next morning, weak from such treatment but surely heartened by the angry murmuring of the spectators, who once more had to be silenced by the crier upon pain of imprisonment. On this fourth and final return the jury did bring in a proper verdict: the two prisoners were simply *not guilty*. The court ordered the jury to be polled, and each man answered "Not guilty," to the great and doubtless noisy satisfaction of the onlookers. Again the Recorder yielded to the stupidity of his instincts, saying to the jury that he was sorry they had followed *their own judgments and opinions* rather than *the good and wholesome advice which was given them;* and for this contempt the court fined them forty marks a man, and ordered them imprisoned till they paid.

Penn, sensing the drama of the moment, stepped in front of the bench. "I demand my Liberty," he said, "being freed by my Jury." The Mayor told him he must first pay his fine for contempt of court in not removing his hat during the trial.

"Take him away, take him away, take him out of the court," shouted the Recorder.

"I can never urge the fundamental laws of England," Penn answered, "but you cry 'take him away, take him away.' But it is no wonder, since the Spanish Inquisition hath so great place in the Recorder's heart. God Almighty, who is Just, will judge you for these things."

Eight of the jury, those who originally would have gone along with the Crown, paid their fines; but the four who had dissented, "phenatique jurymen" as they were dubbed, led by the "pertinaceous" Bushell, brought a writ of *habeas corpus* in the Court of Common Pleas. Twelve judges sat (showing that the government considered the case of great importance), and agreed without dissent that the prisoners should be discharged, since "there was not cause of fine or imprisonment."

The opinion was delivered by Sir John Vaughan, Lord Chief Justice. He carefully examined the functions of judges and of juries. A court cannot tell whether the evidence is full and manifest, or doubtful, lame and dark, he said. However manifest the evidence was,

if it were not manifest to the jury and they believed it not, it was not a finable fault, not deserving punishment. Why should a juror be imprisoned for abiding by his own oath and integrity? To say that a jury acquitted contrary to the instructions of the court in matter of law is not intelligible. "We must take off this vail and colour of words . . ." What use would a jury be otherwise? "The Judge's direction should be hypothetical and not positive . . . If you find the fact thus—then you are to find for the Plaintiff; but if you find the fact thus, then it is for the Defendant."

"If it be demanded," the Chief Justice continued, "what is the Fact? the Judge cannot answer it . . ." Juries like judges may differ as to the reasons for their result.

The learned justice cited a case where a juryman disagreed with his fellows for two days, and, being asked by the judges if he would agree, said he would die in prison first; whereupon he was committed and the verdict of the eleven was taken. But "upon better advice," the verdict was quashed, and the dissenting juror discharged without fine. The juror who disagreed in judgment only was not to be fined. To send such a man to prison seemed unworthy of a court. Accordingly, the prisoners were discharged.

Among the several pamphlets about the trial, one, very brief, published in 1719, purported to be written by Penn and Mead. It was now established, the pamphlet pointed out, that "Judges, how great soever they may be, have no right to fine, imprison or punish a jury for not finding a verdict according to the direction of the Court." "And this, I hope," the writer concluded, "is sufficient to prove that jurymen may see with their own eyes, hear with their own ears, and make use of their own consciences and understandings in judging the lives, liberties or estates of their fellow subjects"—a succinct yet eloquent summary of Vaughan's opinion.

The anonymously written reply, reflecting the point of view of the Crown, should be noticed. *The Answer to the Seditious and Scandalous Pamphlet, Entitled the Tryal of William Penn and William Mead,* by A Friend of Justice, written in the biassed language of a sycophant of the government, though addressed to "the impartial and ingenious reader," supported the prosecution. Penn, the anonymous author said, had blasphemed the Holy Trinity, and in his account of the trial had vilified and contemned the King's court, and reviled all methods of law and forms of indictments, calling them "detestable juggles." "Now, gentlemen of the Long Robe," the author warned the members of the legal profession, "look to yourselves and your Westminster Hall . . . Farewell then to your great acquisitions, your Yearbook will then be out of date. These are the Beasts of Ephesus that the late Lord Mayor, Recorder, and Bench of Justices have been contending withall . . . Justices are but cyphers if they cannot correct the corruption or misdemeanor of jurymen." That "Light" which the Quakers say is within them, is "the Spirit of the Devil, the Father of Lies."

Penn and Mead, like the four jurymen, had been sent to Newgate for nonpayment of their fines. Immediately Penn wrote his father, who was near death, that he and Mead had been declared not guilty, but that the Mayor and Recorder "might add to their malice, they fined us . . . for not pulling off our hats and kept us prisoners for the money, An injurious trifle which will blow over, or we shall bring it to the Common Pleas, because it was against law, and not by a jury sessed." He wanted his father not to worry, but, knowing the elder Penn would want to pay the fine, he could not help adding (in another letter): "I intreat thee not to purchase my liberty . . . I would rather perish than release myself by so indirect a course as to satiate their revengeful, avaricious appetites. The advantage of such freedom would fall very short of the trouble of accepting it." He ended, touchingly: "Let not this wicked world disturb thy mind, and whatever shall come to pass I hope in all conditions to prove thy obedient son." But Sir William had already written to the King, who, along with the Duke of York, promised to continue their favor to young Penn. The Admiral paid the prisoners' fines, and they were released. At the end of his life Penn's father, knowing he was looking into the face of death, forgave his son and at last understood him. He was deeply moved by William's letter. "Son William," he wrote, "if you and your friends keep to your plain way of preaching, and keep to your plain way of living, you will make an end of the priests to the end of the world. . . . Bury me by my mother. Live all in love." Father and son at last had been reconciled.

The son was out in time to be present at his father's death on September 16, 1670. Sir William made him his residuary legatee and sole executor, and bequeathed to him the gold chain and medal that had been bestowed upon him by Cromwell.

William Penn left many memorials behind him: a reputation for fair dealing with all kinds and conditions of men, a clear call to religious liberty, and the "Holy Experiment" in America that became the great proprietorship, colony, and commonwealth of Pennsylvania. But not the least of his accomplishments was recorded in London, in a tablet erected in the Sessions House to the memory of two brave defendants, Penn and Mead, and two stout jurymen, Veer, the foreman, and Bushell. A hundred and fifty years after the trial, the Marquis de Lafayette gave a toast in Philadelphia to the memories of Penn and Franklin—"the one never greater than when arraigned before an English jury, or the other than before a British Parliament."

And so we leave William Penn, "the wild colt," who had just begun his long career of protest. A few months after the trial he would again be arrested for preaching and brought by the soldiers before a huddle of magistrates, this time without jury. Again he would be sent to the Tower. But now the soldiers were friendly and polite. "Send thy lackey," Penn said to the lieutenant, "I know the way to Newgate." There, as usual refusing to pay for special quarters, he wrote several tracts, among them *The Great Case of Liberty of Conscience,* discussing the recent trial; protested to Parliament with the other Quaker prisoners about the stiffening of the Conventicle Act; and dispatched a letter to the sheriffs of London giving them the details of their "common stinking jail."

He was out again in six months.

Francis Biddle was Attorney General of the United States during World War II and afterward served as U.S. judge at the first Nuremberg trial. An honorary Bencher of London's Inner Temple, he is the author of a two-volume auto-biography, A Casual Past *and* In Brief Authority, *excerpts from which have appeared in* AMERICAN HERITAGE.

Suggestions for further reading are difficult, since Mr. Biddle's sources were such rare volumes as Bushell's Case, The Reports and Argument of that Learned Judge Sir John Vaughan, Kt. (London, 1706). For Penn's early career the author drew on Catherine Owens Peare's excellent William Penn, a Biography (J. B. Lippincott, 1907).

READING, WRITING, AND HISTORY

By BRUCE CATTON

The Turning Point

One of the haunting riddles of the American Civil War is the question of identifying its real turning point. It began as a simple struggle between two sections, and it became enormously complex, involving a lasting change in American society; as it changed, it ceased to be a war in which the Southern Confederacy could win its independence by one decisive stroke of arms and became one in which Confederate success depended on a dogged tenacity that would finally induce a war-weary North to give up the contest. To the end, the war remained one which the North could always lose, but somewhere along the line it became one which the South of its own efforts could no longer win. When and where did this change occur?

The natural place to seek an answer, of course, is in the mind of the soldier who knew most about it, General Robert E. Lee. This man of keen military intelligence never deceived himself in the least degree, and he obviously knew, long before the end, that the power to force a decision had passed out of his hands. But he kept his own counsel, then and thereafter.

On the painful retreat to Appomattox, Lee did say that he had never believed the Confederacy could win without help from Europe, but he did not enlarge on the remark and it is possible to suspect that it meant less than it seems to mean. To destroy the Army of the Potomac in one blow would of course have brought European recognition, but that recognition would have been a by-product of climactic victory

rather than a cause. Once it had been possible to hope for such a victory; finally it was not; and although Lee must have known when the change came, he never told anyone about it. He just kept on fighting.

Clifford Dowdey, the able student of the history of Lee's great Army of Northern Virginia, considers the riddle in a thoughtful new book entitled *The Seven Days: The Emergence of Lee,* and suggests that the one great moment of Confederate opportunity came earlier than is generally supposed—not at Antietam and not at Gettysburg, but in the tangled, bloody series of battles fought in front of Richmond at the end of June, 1862, the battles that are referred to now simply as the Seven Days.

Actually, the Seven Days were six, running from June 26 through July 1. There was a skirmish on June 25 and a smaller one on July 2, and nobody really counted either one. The reverberating battle is remembered as "The Seven Days" and it might as well be accepted that way. An extra day's violence somehow got inserted.

During these seven days Lee won a prodigious victory, repulsing the powerful offensive of the Federal General George B. McClellan and compelling McClellan's Army of the Potomac to retreat to a cheerless camp at Harrison's Landing, on the James River, thirty miles downstream from the Confederate capital. The victory had far-reaching consequences—it may well have kept the war going two years beyond its natural course—and it was so startling that McClellan soon persuaded himself that simply by escaping destruction he had accomplished something remarkable; but it left Lee disappointed. This one time he had thought that he could sweep the opposing army clear off the board, and he probably was right. It could have happened. The trouble was that neither Lee nor his army was quite ready for it.

Lee's objective in the Seven Days, in short, was vastly different than it was at Antietam and Gettysburg; which is to say that it was unlimited. Both of his invasions of the North actually had rather limited aims. They were planned as moves that would take the war for a time out of Virginia, throw the Federals on the defensive, open the opportunity for successful maneuvers, and, just possibly, lead to an important victory on Northern soil. But in the Seven Days Lee went all out. Here there was a chance to destroy the Army of the Potomac root and branch, and from the moment of its inception Lee's strategic plan tried to exploit that chance to the uttermost. The chance never quite returned. To win the war with one blow was impossible once this chance was gone.

Background for Crisis

Naturally, Mr. Dowdey addresses himself to the question of how it all happened. Here, although he is working ground familiar to most Civil War students, he brings to an encyclopaedic knowledge of the facts a freshness of insight that makes the story seem new. If the tale has been told before it easily bears retelling, and although he does not labor his point unduly Mr. Dowdey never loses sight of the fact that behind his account of troop movements, bloody combats, and the errors of commanding generals there lies a picture of the nation's greatest war reaching and passing its high moment of change. Here, not quite recognized at the time, was the moment of crisis. After McClellan's beaten army retired to Harrison's Landing, there was a different kind of war.

It was different chiefly because it was going to be longer. If McClellan had dispersed Lee's army the war would have ended then in a final Northern victory, and if Lee had destroyed McClellan's army there would have been a Southern victory, but either way the war would have been over. The revolutionary overturn that always lay just beneath the surface could have been averted, or at least muffled, and whether they remained one country or split into two, the people of America might have gone on much as they had gone before. But the thing had to end. If it went on, the war (having generated its own terrible pressures) would become harder, grimmer, more all-consuming, turning into something that could not be settled by a compromise but that must be fought out to a finish, continuing until one side or the other could fight no

longer. The steamy June days that made soldiers of both sides so uncomfortable in the Chickahominy swamps were probably the last days in which the Civil War could have been kept an incident rather than an explosion.

Mr. Dowdey traces it from the beginning. Early in the spring of 1862 McClellan had taken his army to the tip of the Virginia peninsula and had begun to move up toward Richmond. Opposing him was the Confederate General Joseph E. Johnston—courtly, winsome, able to get along with everybody except his lawful superiors—commanding a much smaller army. Like McClellan, Johnston distrusted his government and was by it distrusted, and he faded back before the invasion without bothering to tell Jefferson Davis what he finally proposed to do. At the beginning of June, with his army arrayed along the Richmond suburbs, Johnston lashed back in the dual battle of Seven Pines–Fair Oaks: a bungled battle that settled nothing, its chief result being that Johnston was wounded in action and was replaced by General Lee.

Lee was no man for a passive defensive. He was as savagely aggressive as any soldier America ever produced, and when he took over, his one thought was to find the best way to smite this Yankee army where it would hurt most. McClellan, who was no more aggressive than Johnston had been, played into his hands. His army of more than 100,000 men was arrayed with 70,000 south of the Chickahominy, facing Richmond, and 30,000-and-odd resting on the north side of the river protecting the right flank and the supply line, and for the rest of June this host remained more or less inert. Some day—when the roads dried, when reinforcements arrived, or when the phase of

---

The Seven Days: The Emergence of Lee, by Clifford Dowdey. Little, Brown and Company. 265 pp. $6.75.

---

the moon was propitious—McClellan would mass everybody, wheel up his siege guns, and break a hole in the Confederate defenses. Meanwhile he would wait until all things were ready.

Lee refused to wait. He struck first, on June 26, hitting McClellan's right at Mechanicsville. Lee had perhaps 75,000 men in all; he left between 20,000 and 25,000 south of the Chickahominy, to contain three times their number, and took everybody else across the river to crush McClellan's right wing. The danger, of course, was that McClellan would catch on, break through Lee's defenses south of the river, and bring the whole scheme to disaster. But McClellan let himself be deceived, and although Lee's assault at Mechanicsville was beaten back, Lee attacked next day at Gaines' Mill and carried the field. Now McClellan had neither a right flank nor a supply line, and since he was unable to see that what lay between his main body and Richmond was no more than a screen there was nothing for him to do but flee to the security of Harrison's Landing and hope for the best. This he immediately proceeded to do.

The Lost Opportunity

Lee had the game in his hand. McClellan's army was penned in between the James and the Chickahominy, and on the map—and if Lee's army had been what it was a year later—Lee had it in his power to destroy him. He could hang on McClellan's rear, send his advance around to block his retreat, hit him in the flank as he moved, and win a shattering, conclusive victory. He saw it, planned it, ordered it—and learned that as things then stood he could not quite do it.

Part of the fault, as Mr. Dowdey points out, was Lee's. He had commanded this army for less than a month and maneuvering a large army deftly was a skill he simply had not acquired. He had a staff that was almost wholly incompetent for this kind of operation, and he had not yet learned how to make certain that his principal lieutenants actually did the things they were ordered to do. Between army headquarters and the separate divisional commands there was a great deal of slippage; the Lee of the Seven Days had not become the Lee of Chancellorsville.

But most of the trouble came farther down the line. Lee's army was not yet organized in army corps; everything depended on the work of the men who commanded divisions, and some of them just were not up to their jobs. (A singular fact, in this connection, is that the Federal government had enforced a corps command system on an unwilling army commander, but the Richmond government had refused to let its army commander have one. Some of McClellan's corps commanders did their jobs poorly, but Lee had none at all.)

In James Longstreet and A. P. Hill, Lee had two division leaders who worked competently and aggressively. He also had such men as General Benjamin Huger, atrophied by age and long years of old-army routine; John B. Magruder, too excitable to understand what he was up against or to execute his orders properly; Theophilus Holmes, even more atrophied than Huger; and, last but not least, the famous Stonewall Jackson, who brought to the Seven Days a towering reputation and somehow failed to take advantage of any of his opportunities. Among them, the generals

let McClellan get away. They made his retreat costly, they fought him in the swamps and on the hills, they left him feeling that he was lucky to be alive—but they did not destroy him, and the chance to destroy him was there.

The most spectacular failure, because it was the most unlikely, was that of Jackson. He was late in getting to the scene, and his tardiness made Mechanicsville a Confederate setback. His troops went into action piecemeal at Gaines' Mill and failed to strike the hammer blow that was expected. He failed abysmally to hit the Federal flank at White Oak Swamp, letting a large part of the Federal army retreat unmolested across his front; the savage battle of Glendale was fought without him; and at Malvern Hill his men did not pull their weight. If Jackson were judged solely on his performance in the Seven Days he would have to be written off as a soldier of very moderate attainments.

His trouble, as Mr. Dowdey sees it, was simply that he was physically exhausted. He suffered from "stress fatigue" to an extent that temporarily robbed him of his mental and physical powers. Lee apparently recognized this. When he shook up his command after the Seven Days, exiling the Magruders and Holmeses and Hugers to distant fields, he retained Jackson, although for a time he reduced the size of the man's command. But there is no disguising the fact that in this campaign Jackson was a bitter disappointment to him.

And, in the end, the seven-day battle was a disappointment also. Here was the one great opportunity to wind things up, and it came to General Lee before his army was able to take advantage of it. Winning a victory, he did not also win the war; he simply prolonged it; and because it was prolonged it became a very different war than it had been in the beginning. Abraham Lincoln had remarked, not long after the war started, that if it lasted long enough it would probably become "a remorseless revolutionary struggle," and that is precisely what happened; after the summer of 1862 it had to be fought to a finish, so that at last it involved not merely a decision about continued union but a complete reshaping of American society. The Seven Days marked the turning point in the war, and the war itself became a turning point in American history.

So this book is more than just one more account of a bloody battle. It is an examination of one of those critical moments when history goes off on a new course. The Army of Northern Virginia was born then, tested and tempered so that it became an incomparable military instrument—in a war which it could no longer hope to win.

Apple Pie without Apples

By CAPTAIN JOHN R. SIBBALD

Unlike the ladies of the abundant Pennsylvania Dutch country (see "Fill Yourself Up, Clean Your Plate," beginning on page 56), the army wives who followed their officer husbands to the American frontier in the nineteenth century faced difficult problems of supply with respect to niceties of the culinary art. There was always plenty of beef —beef, beef, and more beef. But many vegetables as well as dairy and poultry products were persistently hard to get, and when it came to desserts, the logistics of the situation were sometimes just short of disastrous.

Yet mere circumstances offered no exemption from the demands of military social life. The adobe quarters of Indian-fighting garrisons, furnished with rough, soldier-made tables and chairs, often saw banquets where brass-button protocol was observed as

CUSTARD WITHOUT EGGS OR MILK

6 tablespoons of cornstarch
Essence of lemon
Sugar
Water

Blend water and cornstarch to make it creamy thick when cooked. Add essence of lemon. Sugar to taste. Serve in custard cups.

APPLE PIE WITHOUT APPLES

1 medium can of soda crackers
Essence of lemon
Nutmeg
Sugar
Water

Soak soda crackers thoroughly in water. Then warm until soft. Break carefully but not too fine. Add essence of lemon. Blend in sugar and a great deal of nutmeg; bake in pastry, with a top crust to the pie. You will feel sure it is apple pie (if you do not make it yourself).

punctiliously as it was back in Washington, D.C.

It is not surprising, then, that from the general's wife on down, the ladies soon learned to disguise the meanest ingredients, and to take great pride in their culinary deceptions. When the bride of Lieutenant Faye Roe produced a fine "chicken salad" out of veal, for a supper at Fort Lyon, Colorado Territory, in 1872, she reported that what pleased her most were the compliments from other officers' wives who were reputed to know "how to make more delicious little dishes out of nothing than anyone else." But for classic examples of gastronomic fraud on the American frontier, it would be difficult to outdo these recipes for the banquet favorites of Mrs. James Biddle, wife of the Inspector General at Fort Whipple, Arizona Territory, in 1878.